THE

VOYAGES AND ADVENTURES

OF

VASCO DA GAMA

THE

VOYAGES AND ADVENTURES

OF

VASCO DA GAMA

GEORGE M. TOWLE

GYAN

Published by

Gyan Publishing House
5, Ansari Road
Daryaganj, New Delhi-110002
Phone: 011-47034999, 9811692060
E-mail: books@gyanbooks.com

Distribution Network
gyanbooks.com
India, USA, Canada, UK, Australia, France

ISBN: 978-81-212-9114-9 (PB)
First Published, 1878

2nd Impression 2023

Printed at: Gyan Press, Delhi.

THE VOYAGES AND ADVENTURES
AUTHOR: GEORGE M. TOWLE

VASCO DA GAMA SETS SAIL. Page 31.

YOUNG FOLKS' SERIES.

THE

VOYAGES AND ADVENTURES

OF

VASCO DA GAMA

BY

GEORGE M. TOWLE.

Illustrated.

BOSTON:

LOTHROP, LEE & SHEPARD CO.

PREFACE.

IT is the purpose of the author, in this and the succeeding volumes of the "Heroes of History" series, to present, in as interesting a way as he may be able, the true and exciting stories of some famous voyagers and discoverers whose names are not unknown to young people, but whose deeds and adventures are less familiar. While a vast mass of literature for the young has been published, and is being constantly issued from the press, there seems to be some need of books which at once attract the youthful reader's absorbing interest, and teach him some of the wonderful things that have actually happened in the world; the great discoveries made by dint of dauntless courage, unfaltering perseverance, contempt of obstacles, and sturdy conquest of perils by land and sea; the search for fabled treasures, and hazardous travels among strange and interesting peoples.

The aim of this series is to relate truthfully the romantic and thrilling adventures of the "heroes" who are to form the subjects of the volumes, and to do this in a way that will attract and hold the absorbing attention of the young reader from beginning to end.

Vasco da Gama, the subject of this volume, was in his own day more famous than Columbus. Chosen by accident to make a difficult and dangerous voyage, to sail into unknown and savage regions, and to discover a distant and splendid empire, he fulfilled his task with such glorious success, that, on his return, all Europe rang with his praises. Bold and fearless, full of spirit and enterprise, hot-blooded though just and generous, noble in person, and gracious in manner, no man could be more eminently fitted than he for a perilous journey across stormy seas and amid fierce tribes. His discovery of the way to India around Africa and the Cape of Good Hope was one of the most momentous ever made by man; for during several centuries, and up to the time the Suez Canal was dug and opened, but a few years ago, it was the only sea-route between Europe and India.

His story, as will be seen, is full of striking incidents, of strange adventures, of desperate dangers, and of moving triumphs. Few voyages have been more replete with romance; and his career is now narrated for the first time for the benefit of youthful readers, in the hope that it will amuse some of their leisure-hours, and at the same time afford them an important lesson in history.

CONTENTS.

ILLUSTRATIONS.

VASCO DA GAMA.

CHAPTER I.

THE AGE OF DISCOVERY.

WHEN Christopher Columbus made his famous voyage in 1492, he did not by any means achieve the object for which he set out. His purpose in venturing upon that perilous journey across an unknown ocean was, not to find a new continent, but a sea-route to Asia. It had long been thought that Asia, with all its rich gems, spices, and other treasures, might be reached by sailing westward from Europe. Even as far back as the time of the Greek philosopher Aristotle, there were rumors of a land beyond the Atlantic, which, it was suspected, was no other than India. How to discover this supposed passage to India had been a great puzzle long before Columbus made his daring voyage; and the European nations which had ships, and took pride in their commerce, were all anxious to be the first to find it. When Columbus, therefore, after passing safely through many perils, espied the lovely Island of San Salvador, and afterwards Cuba and Hayti, he felt confident that he had made the long-wished-for discovery, for which he would be envied the world over. He was perfectly sure that he had found Asia, and that India was not far off; and in the voyages he made afterwards, when he discovered Jamaica and the northern coast of what we call South America, he was still more convinced that a little farther search would bring him to the well-known shores of Hindostan. To his dying day Columbus believed that it was one side of Asia, and not a new land, that he had discovered; and he was in so little doubt that he had touched near India, that he called the people of the places where he landed "Indians," — a name by which we still know the early inhabitants of our continent.

It was not until some years had elapsed after Columbus's travels were ended that Europe found out that he had struck upon a new, and before unknown, continent. Meanwhile, the story of adventure, romance, and discovery, which he brought back, the accounts he gave of the beautiful islands and strange people and customs he had found far across the sea, and the great renown which by his voyage he had won, not only for himself, but for the good sovereigns Ferdinand and Isabella, who had so generously aided him in his brave purpose, created the most lively excitement and sensation in Europe. He was overwhelmed with honors, and in every part of Spain he was received as if he had been a great conqueror. Spain was very proud of his achievements, and the other nations were very jealous of the prestige and possessions which she obtained as the result of his success.

Among the sovereigns to whom Columbus, some years before his discoveries, had applied for aid in what then seemed his rash and foolish project, was Dom John the Second, King of Portugal; but his petition was refused. Now, the little kingdom of Portugal had long been the rival of Spain in making discoveries. Indeed, although she was far less rich and less powerful than Spain, she had obtained greater triumphs on the sea.

About eighty years before Columbus's first voyage, there lived in Portugal a brave and enterprising prince, named Dom Henry. He was the fifth son of the reigning king, and, when young, had fought valiantly in the wars against the Moors. When peace returned to his country, Dom Henry, who was an ardent student of geography and astronomy, instead of idling away his time at his father's court, spent it in encouraging and fitting out expeditions of discovery. He had himself visited the northern countries of Africa; and one reason why he turned his attention to voyages was, that he was anxious to find out whence the Moors got so much ivory and gold-dust as he observed them to have, and which, they told him, came from beyond the desert. It is said that the expedition which Dom Henry sent to explore the western coast of Africa in 1412 was the very first voyage of discovery ever undertaken by a modern nation.

After this he fitted out and despatched many expeditions. One of the earliest of these came upon the Madeira Islands; at which the Portuguese captain was rejoiced, for he thought that he was the first European to find them.

The Madeiras had been discovered, however, many years before, and in a very romantic way. It happened that a bright and brave young Englishman, named Robert Machin, fell desperately in love with a young lady of noble family. As he was not her equal in rank, her parents sternly forbade a marriage between them. But she loved him as ardently as he loved her; and, as she persisted in preferring him to all the rest of the world, her father did what was not unusual in those rude days, — shut her up, and had Machin arrested, and thrown into prison. The young man succeeded, after a while, in getting out again; and no sooner did he find himself free than he set his wits to work to devise a scheme for possessing himself of his lady-love. He managed to get one of his friends into her house, disguised as a groom, who apprised her of his real character, and told her the plan upon which her devoted lover had resolved. To this she gave a ready assent. One day she took a ride, attended only by the groom, under the pretence of getting the fresh air. The carriage was driven rapidly to the shores of the

British Channel, near which, by chance, she lived. She got out, hurried into a boat, and was rowed out to a ship, where her lover awaited her.

They put to sea, intending to escape to France: but a strong gale blew the ship out of its course; and they were tossed about for many days, completely at the mercy of the waves.

At last they were overjoyed to perceive land not far off. When they had reached it, the lovers went ashore in the long-boat to find themselves on a lovely island; and, as they wandered over it, they came to a spot, under some noble trees, where they resolved to take up their abode with a few of their fellow-voyagers. Some huts were accordingly built, and here the happy couple ensconced themselves.

The ship in which they had come was anchored about three miles from the shore. After they had been on the island for three days, a great tempest arose: the ship was driven from her anchor, and thrown upon the coast of Morocco, where the crew were taken prisoners by the Moors.

When the lovers saw that the ship had disappeared, they became frantic with despair; and so deeply affected was the poor young lady, that she died a short time after. Her devoted cavalier, Machin, could not bear this loss; and he, too, died, begging his companions, with his last breath, to bury him in the same grave with his beloved Anne. The few who remained on the island now fitted up the long-boat with sails, and attempted to regain England; but they, too, were driven upon the African coast, and, like their companions, were captured by the Moors.

In this strange way the Madeiras were discovered by the English, and not by the Portuguese.

Among the discoveries made under the direction of Prince Henry of Portugal were the Canary and Cape Verde Islands, and various countries on the coast of Africa as far south as Lower Guinea. In some places they found gold-dust, ostrich-feathers, and ivory, and other articles of precious value. The ships brought home strange stories of the negroes, as well as rich merchandise.

The passion for discovery in Portugal did not cease with the death of Prince Henry, which occurred in 1463; for, under King John the Second, the Portuguese advanced still farther southward, to the Congo River. All the islands thus discovered off the African coast were taken possession of in the name of the King of Portugal, and attempts were made to colonize them with his subjects. These attempts were, in many instances, successful. An amusing circumstance, however, rendered the Island of Puerto Santo, one of the Madeiras, uninhabitable. In the ship which discovered this island there happened to be a female rabbit, which gave birth to a litter of young rabbits during the voyage. These were let loose upon the island when it was reached, and allowed to remain there; and it is related that the rabbits multiplied so rapidly, that, in two years, they completely overran Puerto Santo, and all idea of a human settlement there was given up. With the negroes on the African coast a brisk trade sprang up; and the fame of Prince Henry, as the "father of discovery," became a household word in his own country and throughout Europe.

King John, the same who refused the aid which Columbus asked of him, was yet resolved that he would find out, if possible, a way to reach India by sea. He had heard that there was a rich and powerful king in India, called Prester John, who was a Christian; and he thought it would be of great advantage to Portugal if he could communicate with him, and secure his friendship. King John knew that the spices, precious stones, and drugs, that reached the rest of Europe through Venice, came from the East; and that it was said that the Venetians brought them from India by way of Aden, in Southern Arabia, Suez, over the country to the Nile, and so up to Alexandria, and across the Mediterranean and the Adriatic.

He accordingly selected two of his most trustworthy courtiers, named Covillian and Payva, and told them to travel as best they could towards India by land, and see if they could find Prester John. The two young men set out, and, going by way of Florence and Alexandria, arrived safely at Aden. Here they separated, agreeing to meet again at Cairo. As they were now uncertain whether Prester John lived in India or Ethiopia, Payva turned his steps into Africa, where, after visiting the court of a sable sovereign who called himself "the Emperor of Ethiopia," and who, Payva thought, might be Prester John, the Portuguese traveller suddenly died. Covillian, meanwhile, pursued his journey from Aden to India, and succeeded in reaching Calicut and Goa. Here he collected a great deal of information respecting India, and was rejoiced to hear that it was possible to reach India around Africa; but he could get no trace of Prester John. So he returned to Cairo, where he heard the sad intelligence of his comrade Payva's death. At the same time he received a message from King John, telling him to continue his search for the Christian king in the East. Covillian seems now to have become convinced, like Payva, that Prester John was no other than the Emperor of Ethiopia; and so he, too, repaired to that sovereign's court. The emperor treated him with great courtesy and kindness, loaded him with presents, and gave him cordial messages for his royal brother of Portugal. Covillian was about to depart with these proofs of the emperor's good will, when the latter suddenly died. His successor was not so kindly disposed; for he would not let Covillian go away at all, but kept him a prisoner for many years, — until his death.

King John never heard of his two faithful explorers again; but the wonderful accounts of India which kept coming to him inspired him with fresh exertions to reach that land of fabulous wealth. Despairing of accomplishing this by a land route, he turned his attention to the discovery of a way to India by sea. It was thought that such a way might be found southward of Africa. The king accordingly fitted up an expedition, and chose Bartholomew Diaz, an officer of the royal storehouse and a vigorous and intrepid man, to command it. Diaz set sail in 1486, and, after encountering many perils, succeeded in doubling the southernmost point of Africa. So frightful were the tempests that raged there, that Diaz named this southernmost point "the Cape of Storms."

When he returned to Portugal, however, and told King John of his discovery, the latter, in his delight, exclaimed, that, since it held out so bright a promise of reaching India by sea, it should rather be called the "Cape of Good Hope;" which is the name it bears to this day.

A strange incident took place during this voyage of Diaz. In one of the most terrific storms his ship was separated from the bark which accompanied him, and which carried the provisions for his crew. At this the men grew desperate, fearing that they would be starved; and threatened to mutiny, unless Diaz should retrace his way home. Diaz, however, persisted, and doubled the cape. Returning homeward, he fortunately fell in with the bark again. But, alas! of the nine men whom he had left in it, only three survived,— such had been their sufferings from cold and famine; and so overjoyed was one of the survivors, Ferdinand Colazza, to see the ship again, that he fell dead at the captain's feet.

It was eight years after the discovery of the Cape of Good Hope by Diaz that Columbus returned with his wonderful story. This filled the Portuguese not only with admiration, but with great alarm lest Spain should get ahead of them in finding a sea-route to the riches of the East. They had every reason to be proud of their daring exploits as navigators; and Columbus's story only inspired King John with new resolution to seek a way to India by water, not westward, as the intrepid Christopher had done, but around the Cape of Good Hope. He longed to win for Portugal the honor and riches which she would gain if her ships were the first to reach India, and he was determined that neither money nor energy should be spared to achieve this exploit.

Such a voyage was certain to be full of perils and difficulties, and many people in Portugal declared that it was an impious tempting of Providence to hazard it. They believed that the storms which Diaz had encountered near the Cape of Good Hope were perpetual, and that no ship could ever pass through them without foundering, or being cast upon the shore, where the voyagers would soon meet with horrible deaths at the hands of savage negroes and cannibals. The king was implored by his superstitious nobles and subjects to abandon the project; and it is greatly to his honor that he persevered in spite of so much eager opposition.

After sending out a foreign merchant named Janifante to coast along Africa and take soundings, — giving him many copper bracelets, brass basins, rattles, bells, looking-glasses, knives, and silks, to give to the negroes, and so conciliate them, — the king ordered his workmen to set to work building three large ships. Wood was cut in the forests, and brought to Lisbon; and the ships that were to undertake the great and dangerous voyage around Africa were forthwith begun.

Unhappily, just at this time the good King John fell ill, and, after lingering for several months, died, without having experienced the joy of seeing his darling project brought to a conclusion. It was fortunate for the Portuguese that he was succeeded by a monarch whose desire to conquer the ocean was not less intense than that of King John; for it was under King Manuel, who now came to the throne, that the thrilling adventures and heroic exploits of Vasco da Gama by sea and land, which are to be related in the following pages, took place.

CHAPTER II.

VASCO DA GAMA IS CHOSEN.

IN the good old times of which we are writing, kings and nobles, as well as the common people, were much given to superstition. They seriously believed all sorts of things which we now see to be absurd. They were credulous, and made a great deal of signs and omens. They were terribly afraid of witches, and thought that their fates could be told by the stars, and that mysterious old men in long black caps, with flowing white beards, were able to foresee future events by muttering strange gibberish, and waving wands, and concocting elixirs and curious potions.

Young Manuel, the new King of Portugal, was by no means free from the superstitious beliefs of his age. He, too, thought that the future could be foretold, and that the stars betrayed the destiny of mortals by their place in the heavens, and the directions in which they moved. Manuel was a hale and vigorous young man of twenty-six when he came to the throne, and his accession was greeted and celebrated with much joy among his people.

This joy was all the greater when they learned that he was fully bent on carrying out King John's purpose of sending out an expedition to find India; for although some of the king's advisers murmured that it would be expensive, dangerous, and perhaps useless, the greater part of the nation approved his design with fervor and delight.

There was living at that time, in a town not far from Lisbon, a swarthy old Jew, named Abraham Cacoto, who was famous for the skill with which he practised astrology. He could tell people, it was said, whether any undertaking would be successful or not, and what their fate in life would be, by consulting the constellations in the heavens.

King Manuel lost no time in sending as secretly as possibly to Cacoto, and bade him come to the palace. Cacoto at once obeyed the royal command; and when he had reached Manuel's cabinet, whither he came disguised and in the night, the king locked the door, and told him why he had sent for him.

"Find out for me, wise Cacoto," said he, "whether the bright stars will bid me to engage in this great discovery. Take your own time, and come and tell me what you learn."

The Jew promised to do so, and went away. Some days after, he returned as secretly as he had come at first. The king saw at a glance that an air of satisfaction rested upon the astrologer's dark and solemn face, and eagerly asked what he had learned from reading the stars.

"Sire," returned Cacoto gravely, with a low bow, "I have bestowed great care upon the task which you have confided to me. I find that India is a long distance from us,—far away over the seas. It is inhabited by dark people; and there are in it great riches and merchandise, that go forth to many parts of the world. There is much danger in going thither: the seas are rough and stormy; there are many savages in the countries on the way, who are full of perfidy and stratagems, and will deceive and try to kill your brave sailors. But, sire, your planet is great under the sphere; and you will discover India, and in no long time you will subjugate a large part of that mysterious land."

This reply, as may be supposed, greatly rejoiced the enthusiastic heart of the young king. He loaded the solemn old Jew with favors, and sent him home amply repaid for his favorable prophecy.

Don Manuel now gave up his thoughts to preparations for the momentous voyage which should bring such glory to himself, and such power to his people. The troublesome counsellors who croaked all sorts of foreboding and disasters in his ear were bidden to hold their peace. The king placed much greater trust in the prophecies of the stars than in their timid wisdom, and no argument was able to dissuade him from his purpose.

The ships which the good King John had ordered to be built still lay but half finished in the dock-yard of Lisbon; while all around were to be seen huge piles of timber cut from the thick forests of Portugal, and now sufficiently seasoned to be used in completing the little fleet.

The sailors who had made the voyage on the African coast with Diaz were employed to do this work, and the king told them to build the ships just as strongly as it was possible to do. Ere many weeks, three goodly vessels, the admiration and wonder of all the people who saw them, lay in their stocks, ready to be launched. They were of the kind called at that period "caravels," such as Columbus had sailed in.

Don Manuel then caused the ships to be supplied with whatever was necessary for so long and dangerous a voyage as they were destined to make; nor were these supplies few or inexpensive.

Each ship was furnished with double tackle, and two sets of sails: and they were also to carry some cannon, and an ample quantity of firearms, powder, and shot; for it was almost certain, that in going among savage nations, and landing upon coasts where they would meet barbarians and cannibals, the crews would need these to defend themselves.

An abundance, not only of provisions, but of preserves, perfumed water, and a whole apothecary's shop of drugs and medicines, was put on board. Besides these, the ships were loaded with a great variety of merchandise, among which were gold, silver, woollen cloths, jewelry, necklaces, chains, and bracelets; silver ewers; yataghans, swords and daggers, some of which were richly and beautifully chased and engraved; spears and shields; and an abundant supply of fine spices.

These things were put in the ships, either to be exchanged for any valuable wares that the Portuguese might find where they should happen to land, or as rich presents to win the gratitude and friendship of the swarthy princes whose realms they might reach.

Don Manuel ordered that each ship should carry two priests and a surgeon; and, in order that the voyagers might be able to communicate with the strange peoples they met, he bought a number of slaves who were thought to be skilled in the languages of the African tribes and the nations of the East.

And now came perhaps the greatest difficulty with which the king had to contend in preparing the expedition. It was to be a most hazardous and formidable journey, and a great deal must depend on the man who should be selected to command the ships. Who was worthy to be intrusted with this momentous duty? Who was there in Portugal brave and intelligent and firm enough to direct the little fleet safely across the tempestuous oceans, and resolute enough to pursue the long journey, despite every obstacle, to the end?

The king gave many hours of anxious thought to this subject, and prayed Heaven to direct him in making a selection so important. His grandees freely gave him their advice, and proposed one man and another as fit to be the captain of the expedition. But to all their suggestions Don Manuel shook his head, and seemed inclined, at last, to leave it to chance to show him the right man for the duty.

Perhaps he was not unwise in this; for chance, or what seemed something very much like it, came to his aid when he was almost at his wits' end.

One morning Don Manuel was sittting in a large hall in his palace, where he was wont to transact the business which it was his daily task to deal with. On a broad table before him were piles of papers, maps, and charts, which he had been diligently studying. His thoughts were still upon the voyage to India, and he was cudgelling his brain for some one to command the expedition.

Grandees, courtiers, and officers of the royal court, were lounging here and there in the hall. Some, in rich costumes, were gathered in groups at a little distance from the king; others were busily bringing in and carrying out papers; yet others, with leisurely gait, were pacing up and down, talking in low tones, and now and then laughing at some sally of wit.

Presently a fine-looking man, about thirty years old, of medium height, with a strong, well-knit frame, very rosy cheeks, a thick brown beard and mustache, and large, dark, clear eyes, came in, and with a firm yet light and easy step sauntered across the hall. He had a decidedly noble and military bearing, and was elegantly attired. By his side hung a sword, and in his hand he carried a velvet cap. It was evident, both from his dress and his manner, that he was a man of rank. Each courtier, as he passed, saluted him with a nod and smile; from which it appeared that he was a favorite at the palace.

As this comely cavalier was crossing the hall, the king happened to look up from his charts and papers. In an instant the troubled expression seemed to leave his face; his eyes were lit up with joy; and he brought his hand heavily down upon the table, as if a sudden and happy idea had just struck him.

"Thank Heaven!" thought the king: "I have found the man!" Then, calling an attendant to him, he exclaimed, "Go and bring to me Vasco da Gama!"

The young nobleman was soon found in an adjoining corridor, and at once obeyed the royal summons.

"Vasco," said Don Manuel, "I have a most perilous and difficult task for you to perform. You know that I have prepared three ships for a voyage to India around Africa. Many an anxious hour have I spent in trying to choose a man capable of commanding them. I know your courage and spirit, Vasco; for they have been tried in the wars in which you have fought so loyally and well. It is you that I choose to discover the way to Africa, which will bring glory to my crown, and riches and power to Portugal. Will you go?"

Vasco da Gama was overcome with surprise, and for a moment looked at the king in speechless astonishment. Here he was, an idle courtier, who had risen that morning with no other thought than how he should "kill time" during the day, selected to perform a journey which even Columbus would have looked upon as dangerous and doubtful!

But he promptly recovered himself, and his mind was soon made up. Bowing low to the king, he replied, "I am your devoted servant, sire; and whatever tasks you confide to me shall be performed while my life lasts."

The king's dinner-hour had now arrived; but so impatient was Don Manuel to talk more with Vasco da Gama, that he bade him follow him in to the table. As they sat at the well-provided board, they conversed eagerly about the expedition.

"I am much bent upon this affair," said Don Manuel; "and I beg you to make ready to depart in all haste."

"As soon as you please, sire," returned Vasco da Gama: "there is nothing to detain me from embarking at once."

"There are three ships," resumed the king. "Who shall be the two captains to go with you? Have you a brother?"

"I have three. One is a small lad; another is studying to be a priest; the third is one to whom your Majesty might intrust any thing."

"And where is he?"

"I am grieved to say, that, just now, my elder brother Paulo, though not a hot-headed man, is in disgrace. He has had an unhappy quarrel with the judge of Setubal, whom he has wounded; and is now in hiding, lest the law should compel him to do restitution. But he is a brave and loyal fellow; and, if your Majesty would pardon him, he would readily accept the service of commanding one of the ships."

"Out of love for you, Vasco, I will pardon him, if he will first satisfy the judge. Tell him to come hither without delay: and do you at once attend to the preparation and equipment of the ships, and choose such sailors as you please; and be assured that you shall have abundant reward for your fidelity."

Vasco de Gama kissed the royal hand, and hastened away to obey Don Manuel's commands. Paulo was not long in making up his quarrel with the judge, and in a few days the two brothers went together before the king.

Don Manuel told Paulo that he had been chosen to aid Vasco in the expedition; and that, although Vasco insisted that he, Paulo, should command it, the king himself desired that Vasco should have that post. It being so arranged, the brothers recommended one Nicolas Coello, a very intimate friend of theirs, to command the third ship; and to this Don Manuel readily assented.

The preparations for the voyage now went rapidly forward. The three ships had already been named the "San Miguel," the "San Gabriel," and the "San Raphael:" and with them was to go a fourth vessel, loaded with provisions; but it was not intended that this vessel should accompany them to the end of the voyage.

Vasco da Gama selected the sailors with great care; and, when he had done so, he told them to make use of the time before the ships set out in learning to be carpenters, rope-makers, calkers, blacksmiths, and plank-makers. For these purposes he provided them with a quantity of tools; and, to their delight, he also increased their pay.

In all, there were about one hundred and fifty sailors. Vasco da Gama himself took command of the "San Raphael;" Paulo da Gama, of the "San Gabriel;" and Nicolas Coello, of the "San Miguel." Large and imposing as these ships seemed to the Portuguese of that day, they were only about one hundred and twenty tons each.

Late in March, 1497, every thing had been got ready; and it now only remained to receive the blessings of the church, to bid adieu to the court and to anxious friends, to leave the scenes and comforts of home behind, and to sail out upon the stormy and unknown seas.

CHAPTER III.

VASCO DA GAMA SETS SAIL.

IT was a bright Sunday morning in spring; and the quaint, narrow streets and spacious squares of Lisbon were full of people.

Something unusual, evidently, was going forward: the old city had the aspect of a holiday, and the multitudes, gayly dressed, were all flocking hurriedly in the same direction.

In the square where stood the ancient and stately cathedral the crowd was most dense and most eager; while, within the edifice itself, a large assemblage, composed of grandees and nobles, of dames and demoiselles, as well as of the common people, filled every niche, aisle, and corner. Behind a curtain which separated them from the rest of the assemblage, the young King and Queen of Portugal, surrounded by a select few of the highest dignitaries of the court, had taken their places; and near this curtain you might have seen Vasco and Paulo da Gama and Nicolas Coello, attired in rich and showy dresses, "the observed of all observers."

At the high altar of the cathedral stood, arrayed in the brilliant costume of his holy office, the Bishop of Lisbon: he was performing high mass, and his voice alone broke the deep silence that reigned in the cathedral.

When he had concluded his prayers, the bishop turned to the assemblage, and told them to pray to God that the voyage of Vasco da Gama might be successful; and went on to utter such praises of the king as were so often sounded in those days from the altars of the churches.

The service over, Don Manuel came out from behind the curtain and spoke to the three captains, who kneeled before him; and the courtiers gathered in a close group around them.

The whole party then repaired from the cathedral to the royal palace, being cheered and saluted on the way by an immense concourse of people.

The time had now come to embark, and soon a procession was formed to proceed to the ships.

Vasco da Gama, having kissed the hands of the king and queen, mounted a fine Arab horse, and put himself at the head of the procession. By his side rode Paulo and Nicholas. Behind them marched, two by two, the crews of the ships, handsomely attired in livery. A large number of noblemen, and officers of the court, accompanied the cortége; a body of monks and priests, bearing wax-candles, and praying aloud, followed; and throughout the route multitudes of people were gathered, many of them weeping at the perils their relatives or friends, the sailors, were about to encounter, others blessing and cheering them on with loud voices.

Arrived at the wharf where the ships lay moored, they found them gayly decked out with ribbons, standards, and flags; and, when Vasco da Gamo appeared, a salvo of artillery welcomed him to the command of his little fleet.

The streets and houses near the wharf were occupied by dense and excited crowds, who filled the roofs and balconies, and were closely packed together down to the water's edge; and so many people were observed weeping and lamenting, that this place was afterward called "the Shore of Tears."

Vasco da Gama now sprang lightly from his horse, crossed the plank with stalwart step, and went on board the "San Raphael," followed by the sailors; and in another moment his resolute face appeared on the deck, gazing upon the familiar scenes to which he was about to bid adieu. His brother Paulo and Nicholas Coello also repaired on board their ships with their men.

Vasco, seeing that all was ready, gave the signal for departure. And now there was seen a busy stir on the decks, while the multitudes on shore remained breathlessly silent.

The sails were spread as if by magic; the anchors were drawn up dripping from the bottom; the cannon on the quays boomed forth a noisy "God speed;" the people shouted, and waved their hands, to which Vasco and his comrades responded warmly from the deck; and the three ships, looking gay and sturdy and gallant in the sunlight, floated smoothly out of Lisbon harbor.

The wind being contrary, the fleet proceeded no farther the first day than the little harbor of

Belem, a few miles westward of Lisbon. Here they anchored until the breezes should be favorable.

Don Manuel accordingly himself repaired to Belem, and took up his quarters in an old monastery there, so as to be near his fleet till it should sail.

Finally, on the third day, a good wind sprang up; and now, at last, Vasco da Gama was fairly off. The king accompanied the ships in his barge out as far as the open ocean, where he took leave of the captains, and watched them until the tips of their masts had faded out of sight beyond the horizon.

The beginning of this momentous voyage was an auspicious one. Fair winds and a quiet sea, blue sky overhead, and a mild and delightful temperature in the air, sped the adventurers on their way. Vasco's spirits ran high; and the songs of the crews, as they climbed up and down the masts, betrayed the gayety of all on board. The three ships and the provision bark kept well together; and often were so near, that the captains could shout to each other so as to be heard.

For a week they thus sailed on, until they were

rejoiced to perceive land, which they soon recognized as the Canary Islands. So far, all was well: they were on the right path. Little did they foresee the dangers through which they would have to pass ere reaching their far-off destination.

Those dangers began, indeed, soon after the Canaries had disappeared from their view. A violent tempest burst upon them, and for hours they were tossed about at the mercy of the waves. When the storm subsided, the "San Raphael," Vasco da Gama's ship, could not be seen anywhere by the others. A dreadful fear took possession of Paulo da Gama and Coello, lest their brave commander had foundered; yet they persevered in their course, making directly for the Cape Verde Islands, as Vasco had commanded in case they were separated.

A week of doubt was ended by the arrival of the ships at Cape Verde, where they were gladdened by the sight of Vasco's standard floating in the wind, and the gallant captain himself standing on the deck. The meeting was celebrated by the firing of cannon and the blowing of trumpets.

The ships now proceeded together to the little Island of San Jago, one of the Cape Verde Islands, where they came to anchor in a snug inlet, and rested there for a week. They seized the occasion to take in fresh water, replenish the ships with provisions from the bark, and repair the yard-arms and rigging that had been injured by the tempest.

A month had now passed since they left; and it must have been about the 1st of May that the ships sailed out of the San Jago bay, and turned their prows, as nearly as Vasco could guess, directly towards the Cape of Good Hope.

Vasco de Gama was full of courage as well as energy. He might have crept timidly along the African coast, and thus delayed his journey for the sake of being more safe. But he was eager to reach and double the cape, and to see what he could discover in the unknown seas beyond: so he stretched at once across the Gulf of Guinea, and held a straight course southward, making long tacks in that direction.

After leaving San Jago, several months elapsed before the eyes of the voyagers were again gratified by the sight of land. Sometimes the sailors became impatient, and were inclined to give up to despair. Sometimes they were deluded by what seemed to be land, but which turned out to be a fog, or a cloud against the horizon. Sometimes Vasco da Gama, consulting his compass and his astrolabe (which was an instrument like our sextant), feared lest he had gone wide of his track. Sometimes frightful tempests threatened to submerge them all in the raging seas.

Still, week after week, and month after month, Vasco da Gama kept resolutely on his course. He had a quick temper; and, when the sailors timidly suggested turning back, he warmly told them that they should go forward until they reached India, or until the sea ingulfed them.

It was late in August when this long voyage across the ocean brought them at last to the southern coast of Africa. The days, they perceived, had become very short; scarcely six hours of daylight enabled them to search for land on the east; while the temperature, after being for a while insufferably hot, had become very cool again.

One morning, land — real land — came in sight; and the ships, which had, singularly enough, been able to keep in sight of each other all this time, ran down upon the coast in the hope of finding a harbor.

In this they did not at first succeed; but, sailing along the shore a little farther, they reached a cosey bay, where they weighed anchor. They named it St. Helena Bay; and Vasco da Gama was sure that they were not far from the Cape of Good Hope.

They were not to leave St. Helena, however, without having some stirring adventures with the dusky natives of that country. Vasco da Gama went on shore with his astrolabe in order to take the altitude of the sun. Meanwhile a number of his men also landed, some to take in water for the ships, and others to stroll about to see what they could find.

While the captain was busy with his instruments, some of his men came hurriedly running to him, and exclaimed, that, as they were ascending a woody hillock near by, they had espied two naked negroes a little distance off, stooping down in the shrubbery as if gathering something.

Now, nothing could please Vaso da Gama better than to hear this; for he was not only curious to see what kind of people lived in Africa, but he was anxious to find somebody who could tell him how near he might be to the cape.

"Go," he said, "and surround them as quietly as possible, and seize and bring them to me."

Five or six men hastened to obey. They crept along, hidden among the brush, until they had got very near the negroes, who, all unconscious of their danger, went on busily with their work. The men now saw that they were gathering honey. They rushed upon them, but only succeeded in capturing one. The other was too nimble, and, in a great fright, ran away.

The sailors returned to Vasco in triumph with their captive, who stared and trembled, and seemed overcome with mingled terror and amazement.

Vasco tried to communicate with him by signs; but he only rolled his eyes, and showed his white teeth, in an agony of fright.

Then a negro boy who happened to be on one of the ships was sent for; and Vasco told him to take the native aside, and to try to get him to eat, and see if he could talk with him. Presently the native became re-assured by the food, and by seeing one of his own color, and now began to make a number of signs and motions with great rapidity, grinning from ear to ear. Vasco dressed him up in gay clothes, gave him some little bells, crystal beads, and a red night-cap, which made him dance with delight; and made signs to him to go and get some of his companions, promising that, when he returned, he should have some more presents.

The native scampered away; and, true to his word, he soon brought back ten or twelve men as woolly and black as himself. These men were small in stature, and as ugly in their features as they could possibly be. They wore the skins of beasts loosely about their bodies, and a queer wooden arrangement about their middle; while for arms they carried oak staves which had been hardened in the fire, upon the end of which horns had been fixed for points. Vasco was amused to observe, that, when they spoke, they made sounds as if they were sighing.

The negroes eagerly took the presents that were offered them, but seemed to care little for gold or silver articles, or for spices: they were much better pleased with toys, tin rings, counters, and beads. But little information could be got from them, however; and so they were sent away.

The next day they returned to the bay, bringing forty or fifty other negroes with them; and these grew so sociable and familiar, that Veloso, one of

Vasco da Gama's men, begged to be permitted to go with them to their village, which by signs they described as being behind a high hill not far off.

Now, this Veloso had a way of bragging a great deal of what he could do; and his comrades were not sorry to see his courage put to the test. Off he started with his new friends, the others cheering him as he went.

Vasco da Gama returned on board the "San Raphael;" while Coello remained on shore to look after the crews while they cut some wood; and Paulo da Gama, who did not like to be idle, took some men in two of the boats, and, provided with fish-spears and harpoons, went out into the bay to catch some fish.

This sport nearly cost Paulo his life. The harpoons had been tied by ropes to the bows of the boats; and, the men having harpooned a small whale, he whirled about savagely, and came near upsetting the boat in which Paulo was. Happily the water was very shallow, and the rope long; so that the monster was with some difficulty taken.

It was nearly sunset, and the captains and men had already taken the boats to return to the ships for the night, when they heard a loud cry from one of the neighboring hills. Turning in that direction, they saw poor Veloso running with all his might towards them.

One of the boats was ordered to return at once to the shore, and take him in; but the sailors, who were not sorry to see the boastful Veloso frightened out of his wits, rowed very slowly, so as to prolong his agony.

The boat touched the shore; and Veloso was on the point of springing in, when a party of negroes rushed out of an ambush where they had concealed themselves, and two of them caught hold of him, and tried to drag him away. A struggle ensued, in which the two negroes were severely wounded with spears. This only enraged the others, who began to hurl showers of arrows and stones at the boat. The other boats hurried up to take part in the fray, and some of the Portuguese jumped on shore. Vasco da Gama, eager to punish the savages for their perfidy, was standing up in his boat, and giving orders to his men, when an arrow sunk its point in his leg. The captain, however, insisted on remaining, and commanded some of his cross-bowmen to pour a volley into the negroes, which they did with good effect. The

ELOSO AND THE SAVAGES. Page 40.

savages ran howling away to their hills, and the voyagers returned leisurely to the ships. Veloso, when once safely on board, told a brave story about his adventures with the negroes; and said that they had intended to use him as a decoy to lure others on shore, and then destroy them. He related, too, how the negroes ate the roots of herbs, gulls, whales, seals, and gazelles; and how they had dogs very much like those at home in Portugal.

It then turned out that the hostility of the natives was due to a blunder of Veloso himself. When he arrived at the negro village, they thought to do him honor by cooking a large sea-calf, which they set before him, in one of their rude huts. He was so disgusted with the smell and look of it, that he rose abruptly, and strode off towards the bay. The natives, in perfect good humor, went with him: but he became frightened on the way; and, as soon as he came in sight of the ships, he shouted so frantically, that he alarmed the negroes, who plunged into the thicket.

They misunderstood his cries, and thought that he was calling upon his companions to come and attack them: hence their assault upon him as he was getting into the boat.

Vasco da Gama now despaired of learning any thing about the Cape of Good Hope from these savages; and only tarried at St. Helena Bay three or four days longer, until his ships could be amply supplied with wood and water.

About the 1st of September the sails were once more spread, the anchors weighed, and the prows turned seaward. A south-west wind carried them briskly along; and, Vasco having told his men in a confident tone that he was certain the cape was not far off, the little fleet set forth cheerily on its way around the continent.

CHAPTER IV.

VASCO DA GAMA DOUBLES THE CAPE.

ALTHOUGH Vasco da Gama had learned nothing from the black natives of St. Helena, he felt very sure that it would not be long before they saw the Cape of Good Hope. The cape was, indeed, not far off; but the gallant little fleet had to pass many anxious days, and encounter many dreadful hardships, before they could double it.

Scarcely had they emerged from the tranquil harbor of St. Helena when the ships were struck by contrary winds and tempestuous weather. The waves soon rose to a prodigious height, and tossed the poor little vessels about as if they were frail playthings made for the savage amusement of the sea. Now they seemed to be hurled up among the clouds; then the sailors trembled lest the furious waters which they saw raging far above them on every side should ingulf them forever in the deep. The wind was not only furious, but chilling cold. The pilots could not shout loud enough to make their orders heard by the sailors, so deafening was the uproar of the storm.

After brief periods of daylight, a long and dreadful darkness would hang over them, and prevent their seeing in what direction they were going. The masts and shrouds were stayed; and the ships, no longer to be controlled, drifted whithersoever winds and waves compelled them. It was now that the heroic resolution, courage, and constancy of Vasco da Gama were put to the proof. When the storm lulled for a time, his sailors, wearied and despairing, crowded around him, and passionately besought him to give up his purpose, and to turn the prows of the ships again towards home. They begged him to consider that these were the perpetual storms which had always forbidden ships to pass the cape; and they cried out, that, unless he turned back, they should all find watery graves. They declared that the land, which came in sight as often as they tacked to double the cape, had no end, but extended to the Antarctic Sea; and again and again they pleaded, as if for their lives, with their obdurate captain.

But Vasco da Gama was not to be moved. At first he chid his men gently, and said to them, —

"I assure you, good fellows, the cape is very near. Do not despair. If we keep tacking, we shall surely double it."

He set them a good example by freely and cheerfully sharing their dangers and hardships. Promptly, at the sound of the boatswain's whistle, Vasco da Gama appeared on deck with the others. He seemed never to take any repose, but was here and there and everywhere, often remaining day and night at the helm, ordering the men, and seeing to it that nothing was left undone. He ate the same coarse fare that was allotted to the humblest sailors; and, when the pilot was exhausted, Vasco himself took his place.

Finally, however, he lost patience, and grew very angry at the importunities of the men. Gathering them all on deck, he sternly told them that he would stand out to sea until the cape was doubled, or until the ships went down.

They had been making as many tacks to the windward as the storm would permit; but, every time they returned again towards land, they were disheartened to see the long and irregular coast re-appear in the east.

At last Vasco da Gama resolved that he would make a long tack, and stand on it until it was certain that he could double the land.

The storm was now gradually subsiding. The caravels sped somewhat more easily on their way; and, after a few days, Vasco ordered the sailors to once more turn the prows towards the continent. As they slowly sped south-eastward, prayers to Heaven went up from all the decks, and both captains and sailors seemed to take more heart. The ships labored less and less; the sea grew calmer; and through the long nights and brief days the brave little vessels, showing each other colored lights at frequent intervals, so as not to part company, kept steadily on.

This time no land appeared; and Vasco da Gama ordered the ships to sail more free, in order, if possible, to espy it. One morning they awoke to find themselves floating on a tranquil sea, with a gentle wind wafting them forward.

It was a pleasant morning, very unlike the many wretched, dismal days they had passed; and now, though they had seen no land, Vasco knew that they had doubled the cape.

The other two ships were signalled to come near the "San Raphael," and the glorious news was shouted from deck to deck.

Both captains and sailors gave themselves up to the most eager demonstrations of joy. Some climbed the masts, and waved their caps to each other from ship to ship; some ran and got trumpets, which sent a joyous din of sound over the serene and sunny sea; some could only show their delight by firing off cannon; and some wildly embraced each other, and danced about the deck. All the dangers and troubles of the past were forgotten in a moment; and as Vasco da Gama, his handsome face flushed with triumph and pleasure, strode up and down among his men, they kissed his cloak, and prayed for his pardon, and showered blessings upon him. They little knew that it would not be long before the keenest despair would again seize them, and incite them to make a murderous attempt upon their brave captain's life.

A solemn quiet suddenly succeeded the joyful noise of shouts, singing, cannon, and trumpets. Arrayed in their robes, the priests appeared upon the decks. With one accord every man dropped upon his knees, pulled off his cap, and bent low his head; and then, amid the stillness, the solemn voices of the priests were raised, repeating the "Salve," and uttering to God the gratitude with which the hearts of all were filled to overflowing.

The little fleet now cheerily resumed its journey, and one morning they caught sight of some lofty mountain-peaks. To Vasco's delight he perceived that the land was no longer east, but north of him. Irregular ridges, blue in the distance, lined the horizon; and here and there jagged promontories ran boldly out into the sea.

Vasco directed his ships towards the shore, and skirted it leisurely during the night. At dawn they saw pretty sandy beaches interspersed with rocks, glistening in the sunlight; while coves, streams, and even good-sized rivers, appeared at intervals. The crews amused themselves with spearing fish, which they cooked; but the fish made the men who ate them sick, and the sport lost its attractions.

After running along the coast for three days amid a balmy air and beneath a sunny sky, they came to the mouth of a large river. Vasco da Gama ordered the sailors to lower a boat, and reconnoitre the shore. No natives were anywhere to be seen. The mouth of the river having been sounded, and proving to be twelve fathoms deep, the ships entered it, and cast anchor.

Vasco da Gama, for the first time since they had left St. Helena, went on board his brother Paulo's ship; and Nicolas Coello, the other captain, soon joined them. The three captains embraced each other fervidly; and then, sitting down to a well-provided table which Paulo had prepared, they talked about the dangers and adventures they had passed through, and made merry over their safe arrival on the other side of Africa.

The Portuguese, meanwhile, landed upon the banks of the river, and, dividing themselves into little groups, wandered about to see what they could discover. How refreshing it was to find themselves once more upon the firm land, after all the hardships of the last two months! How pleasant to see the green grass, and to quaff the sparkling waters of the streams, after the weary monotony of the sea, and the scant fare to which they had been subjected!

They found, however, nothing remarkable; nor were any human beings anywhere to be seen. It seemed a deserted coast; and, after putting in wood and fresh water, the ships sailed away again.

A few days after, still hugging the coast, they came to another and larger bay, which Vasco da Gama named San Blas. It seemed to invite them to enter, being a sheltered nook, and apparently an inhabited spot. On the rocks overlooking the bay they observed thousands of seals, with long white teeth and ferocious aspect, warming their sleek fur in the sun.

Vasco da Gama thought this a good place to take a rest; and the ships were, therefore, anchored in the bay. The store-ship which they had brought with them was here emptied of its provisions, which were divided among the other vessels; and the storeship itself was burned.

The men had not been long on shore before they came back with exciting reports of the strange animals they had met with. They said that they had seen enormous elephants wandering about, and very fat oxen without horns. On the rocks they had espied many large birds, which seemed to have no feathers in their wings, and which uttered a grating cry like the braying of asses.

Presently they discovered that the country round about was inhabited. They caught sight of a number of black fellows, almost naked, riding about in the distance on the backs of the fat oxen; and, after the ships had been in the bay several days, bands of sooty natives appeared, capering about in an excited manner on the rocks, pointing to the strange vessels, the like of which they had never seen before, and gesticulating wildly to each other.

Vasco da Gama was resolved not to be caught in the same trap into which he had fallen at St. Helena. He was anxious to converse with the natives, and find out, if possible, where he was; but he had learned to be cautious. So he ordered the men to arm themselves well before going on shore; and to carry some cannon with them, in case they should be needed. The negroes grew gradually bold enough to come along the beach, pretty near the ships; and Vasco seized the opportunity to throw out to them some little bells. The savages caught them up, and went scampering over the beach, ringing them, and making a great ado. Then the others became confident, and approached near enough to take the bells from Vasco's hand, grinning at him, and then dancing about.

He was surprised and pleased to find them so familiar, and, telling his men to bring him some red night-caps, found no difficulty in going among the natives, and exchanging them for the ivory bracelets which they wore on their arms.

The next morning the shore was fairly swarming with black men, women, and children, almost naked, who rushed to and fro, and crowded, with eyes wide open, around the ships. Vasco, the other captains, and the men, went on shore, and fearlessly mingled with the sable crowd; and, to their surprise, they were regaled with a number of roasted oxen and sheep, which the natives had brought with them, and which they cooked on the beach after their barbarous fashion.

Invited to partake of these welcome dishes, the Portuguese willingly complied; and a merry time they had of it all day long. The negroes enlivened the feast by playing on flutes made of reeds, and singing songs in a strange, screeching way that caused the Portuguese to laugh heartily. The latter returned the compliment by blowing their trumpets, which seemed to fill the natives with astonishment.

Vasco da Gama seized the occasion to buy some of the sheep and oxen. While he stood bargaining for them, two or three of his men hurried up to him, and told him that they had just seen some young negroes suspiciously hidden in the bushes.

He at once ordered his men to retreat near the ships; seeing which, the natives gathered menacingly and quickly in a close group, as if they intended to attack the strangers. Vasco was unwilling to harm them, however, and gave a sign to the crews to go on board. When everybody was safe in the ships, he ordered two cannon to be fired over the heads of the negroes. The loud and sudden report overcame them with surprise and terror; and, dropping their weapons on the beach, they ran away into the bushes as fast as their naked legs could carry them.

Vasco, before leaving San Blas, erected a pillar on the shore, bearing the arms of Portugal, as a token that he had taken possession of the bay in the name of King Manuel; but, as he was about to set sail, he had the mortification to see the negroes come and pull it down, and defiantly throw it into the sea.

CHAPTER V.

VASCO DA GAMA QUELLS A MUTINY.

IT was not to be all fair sailing in calm seas, however, and pleasant sojourns in cosey bays. Many a league across the uncertain waters had yet to be crossed ere the intrepid Vasco da Gama reached his goal. Dangers were to multiply, and he was called upon to use all his stern resolution and dauntless courage to overcome them. The perils he had passed —perils of storm, and perils among savage races —were to be again endured; and other perils, quite as formidable, were to be added to them.

But his stout heart quailed before no threat of men, or of the elements: he looked forward to the future as cheerfully as he exulted in the difficulties he had already overcome.

An event was about to happen which would

test his courage, and presence of mind, to the utmost.

After entering several other bays, and finding nothing to satisfy their curiosity, or make it profitable to land, the caravels put out into the open sea again. In the daytime they ran under full sail as long as the wind would permit them, while at night they proceeded more slowly and cautiously. More than once they were becalmed, and had to lie by until a breeze sprang up; and, as they drifted farther away from the continent, they began to find that they had by no means left the storm region behind, when they doubled the cape.

It was now winter. The voyagers were yet far from their destination, but how far they knew not; and the sudden storms of that season of the year were not tardy in assailing them.

One morning a terrific tempest burst, almost without warning, over their heads. Vasco da Gama took his place on deck, and, rapidly scanning the heavens with his keen eye, gave his orders rapidly and clearly. "Make the masts fast with ropes, my men!" he shouted. "Pass the shrouds over the yards! You two, take the pannels off the tops and sails! Strike all sails except the foresails: we'll weather the storm with them!"

Cheerily the men set about the tasks commanded by their captain: but, as they labored, the tempest grew yet more furious; until at last the pilot, doffing his cap, came up timidly to Vasco, and said, —

"I fear the ships are not strong enough to weather this tempest, captain. Let us put in to land, run along the coast, and find a secure haven till the storm is over."

"No!" cried Vasco. "Return to your post, pilot! When I came out of Lisbon harbor, I swore not to turn back a span's breadth. Whoever again proposes to return on our track shall be thrown into the sea, to be food for fishes!"

The crew looked at him aghast; but his countenance was stern, and they could find in it no sign that he would relent.

The gale was all this time increasing, and fitfully veered in every direction; the waves were running to a frightful height, and, falling, drenched the decks with floods of water. Then the wind suddenly lulled, so that the ships lay helpless on the surging sea, and lurched so badly, that they took in water on either side.

The men were forced to tie themselves fast to the masts and rigging to save themselves from being washed overboard. It became almost impossible to work at the pumps; and the ships creaked so noisily, that it seemed as if they would go to pieces at any moment.

The sailors now became more piteous in their appeals to Vasco da Gama to turn back; but he grimly replied, —

"I have said that I would not; and, if I saw a hundred deaths before my eyes, I should go straight on. To India we shall go, or perish." Then he added, in more persuasive tones, "Think of the honor and rewards our good king will shower on us when we return with the story of our exploits! Come, my men, pluck up courage, and put your faith in God."

It happened, that, when the little fleet sailed from Lisbon, five or six men, who had been condemned to death for various crimes, were released, and put on board. The object of this was, that Vasco da Gama might use these convicts to explore dangerous places, and thus not risk the lives of his sailors. The lives of the criminals were looked upon as worthless; and, if they were killed by savages, it mattered little.

These men, when they saw the crews abandoning themselves to despair amid the tempest, and Vasco da Gama resolute in his purpose to go forward, thought it a good opportunity to make mischief.

They got together at the end of the "San Raphael," and began to whisper among themselves; and presently, calling some of the other sailors to them, muttered mysteriously in their ears.

Just then the tempest lulled a little, so that the three ships could approach within speaking distance of each other. The sailors on the "San Raphael" began to shout to their comrades on the "San Gabriel" and the "San Miguel," and to incite them to resist the orders of the captains.

Vasco da Gama thereupon cried out to his brother Paulo and to Nicolas Coello that he would on no account turn back to the coast, and told them to keep bravely on their course. Some of the sailors on the "San Miguel" were so bold as to cry out angrily that they were many men, while the captain was but one; thus betraying their disposition to mutiny.

A sudden wind fortunately arose, and the ships

were again separated. Deafening thunder pealed across the skies, and a dense darkness enveloped them. The ships, however, hung out lights, so that they might not lose each other; for Vasco da Gama feared, that, if they should part, the sailors would take forcible possession of the caravels, and put back to Portugal.

Such a plot was, indeed, going forward in all the ships, instigated by the criminals who had been brought along in them; and their design would probably have succeeded, had it not been for the imprudence of one of the men on the "San Miguel," who divulged the conspiracy to his brother, a young boy, who was Nicolas Coello's attendant.

This boy was devotedly attached to his master. Concealing his intention from his brother, and promising to keep the secret, he took the first occasion to warn Coello of the danger which threatened the fleet. Coello made up his mind that he would die before he would permit the mutineers to seize him, or get control of the ship. Arming himself to the teeth, he watched their movements day and night, and told his faithful attendant never to lose sight of the ringleaders, but to find out all he could of their intentions, by winning their confidence, and seeming to enter into their plans.

Soon the boy came to him with the news, that the men proposed to wait until they could act in concert with the sailors on the other ships before rising in mutiny. Meanwhile Coello, dissembling his fears and speaking gently to his men, bethought him of a way to let Vasco da Gama know what was going on, without giving the alarm to the conspirators.

Several days passed; and when, amid the raging of the storm, his sailors still urged Coello to leave Vasco to his fate, and turn back, he replied, —

"I promise you, that, as soon as I can speak to the captain, I will demand of him to put back, and bring us safe home again."

The storm became less furious; and the sea grew so calm, that the ships could once more approach each other. Coello, as soon as he was within speaking distance, shouted to Vasco da Gama, —

"I beg you, captain, let us turn about, and make for Portugal again. The men are begging to go back, with tears in their eyes; and, if we do not yield to them, they will be tempted to seize and kill us. We ought to yield to them; and, if we do not, you must look out for yourself, captain, as I am going to do."

Coello cried loud enough for both Vasco and Paulo to hear.

Vasco da Gama, when there was another lull, cried back, "Well, Coello, I will consult my pilot and crew, and will signal to you when I have made up my mind."

The quick-witted captain had understood Coello, though the mutineers had not. He knew that Coello meant to give him warning of a mutiny. Perceiving that he must conceal his real intentions, and pretend to yield to the clamor of the crew, he called them together, and told them, that, if another tempest should arise, he would put back.

"But first," he added, "you must sign a paper, giving the reasons why we abandoned our voyage, so that our good king's anger may be appeased."

The men cried out with one accord, overwhelming Vasco da Gama with their thanks and praises, and eagerly promising to sign whatever he wished.

"You need not all sign," replied Vasco. "It is only necessary for those to do so who best understand the guiding of the ships and the difficulties of the sea. Pick me out such men, pilot, and they shall sign."

Vasco da Gama went into his cabin with his clerk, taking the precaution to station a faithful sentinel at the door. The document was speedily drawn up; and Vasco da Gama told the clerk to take it below to the store-cabin, which was underneath his own.

"Tell the pilot and the master," he said, "to go down there and sign it."

No sooner had those officers descended, than, to their speechless astonishment, they found themselves seized one after another, roughly thrown down, and put in irons.

The sailors staid on deck, ignorant of the fate of their comrades. It remained to seize the men who had been designated by the pilot and master as skilled seamen. These were called, one by one, into the captain's cabin; and, before they knew it, irons had been clapped upon them, and they were helpless prisoners.

Vasco da Gama now ordered the pilot, master,

and other prisoners to be brought on deck, and, pointing to them as they stood in a row with dismal faces, said to the rest of the crew, —

"You see how I deal with those who dare to conspire to resist my authority. Take a lesson from these fellows, and see to it that you obey orders, and do not murmur; for, if you do, you will find yourselves in their predicament. Every one of these fellows will remain below deck in irons till we return to Portugal: there they shall be delivered up to the judgment of the king."

Then turning to the pilot, who stood manacled and with head bowed down, the captain continued sharply, —

"You, pilot, — where are your astrolabes, quadrants, and other instruments? Fetch them to me."

The pilot sullenly pointed out the instruments to the men who were guarding him, and they were brought to the captain.

"Here," said Vasco de Gama, holding them up, "are all the means we have to find out where we are, and in what direction we are going. And now," he added, hurling them violently into the sea, "I cast them forth, so that they are lost for-

Vasco Da Gama Quells a Mutiny. Page 64.

ever. I need neither pilot nor master, neither astrolabe nor quadrant. I place my trust in God, who will guide us henceforth. If we deserve it, he will deliver us safely out of the seas to our destination. I will take the place of the pilot who has proved a traitor, and myself will direct the courses of the ship."

This firm conduct completely subdued the rebellious disposition of the crew, who hastened to crave the captain's pardon for their mutinous designs. They begged him to release the men in irons; but to this he turned a deaf ear. He took up his station at the pilot's place, and himself undertook to guide the ship on its perilous way.

When the other two ships again came near, Vasco da Gama told Paulo and Coello what he had done. The crews of the "San Gabriel" and "San Miguel," disheartened by the failure of the crew of the "San Raphael," and won, moreover, by the gentle words of their own captains, who sought to persuade them to abandon their purpose, soon gave over all thoughts of violence; and so the little fleet once more sailed peaceably over the waters.

The long storm had meanwhile greatly damaged

the three ships. Their holds were so full of water, that the pumps seemed to make little impression upon the flood that had gathered in them. In many places the ships leaked, and betrayed sore need of repairs. Many barrels of water had been burst in and broken up; and so the supply of fresh water for drinking had got very short, and the cooks were obliged to use salt water for cooking the provisions.

Vasco da Gama was prudent as well as brave. He saw the necessity of making land, if possible; and ordered the ships to once more turn their prows towards the African coast.

It was not long before land came once more in sight, much to the delight of the crews. They caught sight of a very pleasant landscape, with pretty copses of trees, and sloping hills on which they could see cattle browsing. They passed close to a high and jagged rock, which Vasco called "the Rock of the Cross;" and on Christmas Day they skirted a cape, which, with pious thought, he christened "Natal."

About ten days after this, Vasco da Gama espied the mouth of a large river, and a spacious bay well sheltered from the winds. Here he decided to cast anchor; and so grateful were they all to find themselves once more floating in calm waters, and near the land, that they called the river "the River of Mercy."

CHAPTER VI.

ADVENTURES ON THE COAST.

THE Portuguese wanderers found their new sojourning-place all that could be desired. Although it was January, the weather was temperate and sunny. Vasco da Gama, thinking that he had so far made good progress, was in no hurry to depart; and, as the ships greatly needed repairs, he decided to remain at the mouth of the River of Mercy for several weeks.

The crews were allowed to go on shore as much as they liked. Meanwhile Vasco and Paulo da Gama seized the opportunity to be often together, to talk over the mutiny, and to congratulate each other upon its prompt suppression.

One of the first things the sailors did was to go a-fishing. They caught a large number of curious-looking fish, which proved to be more palatable and more healthy than those caught near the cape. From the river they got very good water; which was a blessing they had long been without, and which they eagerly quaffed, and brought to the ships for cooking the food.

The men then set lustily to work repairing the ships. A broad shelving beach stretched out near by, where they might have drawn the ships aground, and thus mended the leaks; but Vasco thought it a better way to heel them over in the water, and thus careen them.

The "San Miguel," on being examined, proved to be too badly injured for further service: so Vasco da Gama ordered that it should be broken up, and its stores and materials used for replenishing and repairing the other two caravels.

They beached the "San Miguel," took away its rudder, stowed its wood and iron work, and set it on fire so as to get the nails from it.

The next thing was to repair the "San Gabriel," Paulo da Gama's ship, which had also suffered a great deal of damage from the tempests. They managed to heel her over by putting all the stores and heavy materials on one side, by which means they laid her keel bare. Planks were hung up on the outer side, and some of the men employed themselves in scraping off the seaweed which clung to it; while others repaired the leaks, extracted the rotten calking, replacing it with oakum, over which they put a coating of pitch. The pitch was boiled in a boat moored just by.

Then the "San Gabriel" was turned over on the other side, which, being less damaged, was more speedily repaired. When she was turned upright again, she proved to be perfectly water-tight. The stores of the "San Raphael" were now transferred to the "San Gabriel," and the "San Raphael" was then repaired in a similar manner. The two ships were finally refitted inside with new ribs, knees, and planking.

The three captains dined together every day, and had a merry time of it. As they had plenty of time, they resolved to explore the neighboring country. Vasco da Gama accordingly sent Nicolas Coello, with twenty men, on an expedition up the River of Mercy.

After rowing six or seven miles, Coello came upon thick forests, and fields of green turf; and a little farther he found some negroes, not so black as they had before seen, and naked, except that they wore an apron of plaited leaves and grass about their middles. These negroes were fishing. As soon as they saw Coello's boat, they rowed up without a moment's hesitation, and coolly jumped into it. Coello tried to converse with them by signs; but they did not understand him. After looking the white men carefully over, they went back to their canoes. When Coello returned to the bay, one of the canoes followed him; and, arriving at the ships, the negroes boldly went on board the "San Raphael," and sat down as if to rest themselves.

Vasco da Gama treated them as hospitably as the resources of his ship would permit. He gave them some biscuit, cakes, and bread spread with marmalade: but the negroes would not touch these good things until they had seen the Portuguese eat; then they fell to with an appetite, greedily gulping down the food, and angrily refusing to share it with each other.

Vasco da Gama observed that these negroes, both men and women, were not only lighter in complexion than those of St. Helena and San Blas, but were much taller and heavier, with matted or tangled instead of woolly hair. They carried as arms some sticks, the ends of which had been hardened in the fire, and had sharp, greased points.

Soon a whole fleet of canoes was seen coming down the river. When they reached the ships, a multitude of negroes jumped out upon the beach, and eagerly pressed forward to go on board. They did not show the least timidity, and seemed but little surprised to see the ships; from which Vasco da Gama concluded that this was not the first time that large vessels had been upon that coast.

Vasco was too prudent to permit them all to go on board the "San Raphael" at once: so he admitted them ten at a time. Some of the negroes had brought birds and plums; of which the Portuguese, after some hesitation, partook, and found them very nice, the birds being quite sweet and tender. In return, Vasco caused his guests to be regaled with wine and biscuit.

The negroes grew so friendly, that Vasco was inclined to do whatever he could to please them: so he brought out a looking-glass, and gave it to them. They had evidently never seen one before. They stared at it, held it up to their companions, and then roared with laughter to see the faces reflected in it. They kept continually peering into it, and shouting to their companions in the canoes. At last they carried the looking-glass on shore, as delighted with this new wonder as a child with a whistle.

Vasco had completely won their hearts by giving them the looking-glass; for in a few hours they returned in their canoes, bringing a large number of birds, which the sailors killed, and dried in the sun for future eating. The negroes were rejoiced to receive in payment some copper bracelets, bells, rattles, and white cloths; and so grateful were the sailors for the birds, which promised many a feast on the rest of the voyage, that they even tore up their shirts, and distributed the strips among their dusky friends.

It happened that one of the men on board the "San Raphael"—an old sailor named Martin Alonzo—knew a little of the Caffre language, which was spoken on the opposite or west coast of Africa. He was surprised to hear these negroes using words very similar to those of the Caffres; and, on making the attempt, he found that he could talk quite well with them.

The negroes made him understand that they lived in villages some leagues up the river, where their chief or king was, and invited him to go thither with them.

Vasco da Gama was much pleased to find a means of intercourse with these friendly savages. He not only bade Martin go with them to their villages, taking another of the sailors along with him, but gave him a red jacket, a pair of red breeches, and a copper bracelet, to carry as a present to the king.

When Martin returned the next day to his comrades, he had an amusing story to tell. Taking him and his companion in one of their canoes, the natives had rowed them rapidly up the river, paying them many attentions, and chattering to them all the time. They passed through a lovely country of forest interspersed with rich green fields; and here and there they passed graceful slopes, on which Martin saw cattle grazing quite unlike any he had ever seen before.

Arrived at the principal village, he found it composed of low huts made of straw, the interiors of which were cosey and comfortable. Presently the chief of the tribe made his appearance, and greeted Martin with lively demonstrations of good will. Martin made haste to confirm his friendship by giving him the jacket, breeches, cap, and bracelet. The king, on seeing them, danced about with delight, and eagerly arrayed himself in them. Then he strutted proudly about among his people, and went from hut to hut to show off his finery. Coming back to Martin, he told him that he might have any thing the country afforded.

Martin and his companion were then entertained at the chief's hut with some delicious birds roasted at the fire, and a sort of porridge made of millet; which, being hungry, they heartily partook of. During the evening a crowd of negroes surrounded the tent, gazing curiously at the strangers; but finally retired, and left them to enjoy a sound sleep.

Martin described the negroes as being armed with long bows and arrows, and spears tipped with iron. They wore copper ornaments on their arms and in their hair, and had in their girdles iron daggers, with pewter handles and ivory sheaths. They seemed to have an abundance of salt, which they kept packed away in caves. For an old shirt they gladly bartered a large quantity of copper. He observed that among them there were a great many more women than men.

The next morning a fleet of canoes escorted Martin and his comrade back to the ships. From first to last, Vasco da Gama saw or heard of nothing but friendliness, gentleness, and generosity on the part of these natives; and so pleased was he with their amiable conduct, that he called the place "the Land of Good People."

One misfortune attended the sojourn of the ships at the River of Mercy. The scurvy broke out among the crews, and made many of them very ill. This is said to be the first time that this strange disease is mentioned as having attacked European sailors.

Before Vasco da Gama set sail again, he gladdened the hearts of all his men by a generous and merciful act. His brother Paulo, who was a very sweet-tempered and gentle-hearted man, pleaded with him for the pardon of the master, pilot, and other mutineers, who still lay below deck in irons. In this petition Paulo was joined by Coello and the sailors.

"Well," said Vasco, "be it so; but, when I get back to Lisbon, I shall present these men in irons to the king, not to have them punished, but to show him what difficulties have beset me in this voyage."

Then, calling up the prisoners, he ordered the irons to be taken off, and said to them, —

"You are pardoned and free. Beware, however, lest you allow treason to enter your hearts again. Faint-heartedness brings misfortune; but courage conquers the most serious difficulties. Let us put our trust in God, and never falter to our journey's end."

The sailors broke into a loud cheer, and eagerly thanked their captain; and the released prisoners showed their penitence and gratitude by setting to work at once with a will, as if to make up for their past misconduct.

Vasco da Gama set up a marble pillar at the mouth of the River of Mercy, engraved with the arms of Portugal on one side, and a picture of the globe on the other; over which was placed the inscription, "Of the Lordship of Portugal, the Kingdom of Christians."

One pleasant morning they weighed anchor,

and floated out of the river under a brisk land breeze.

Still skirting the coast for some days, the ships again came to anchor at the mouth of a wide stream, now known as the Zambesi, which Vasco called "the River of Good Signs," because here they learned from a young native that he had come from a country a long distance off, away over the seas, where he had seen ships as large as those of Vasco da Gama. This country Vasco believed to be no other than India.

The negroes who visited the ships at the River of Good Signs were as peaceable and friendly as those whom they had just left behind at the River of Mercy. They were naked, except that they wore a cotton band about their middles; while the chief men, or nobles, had handkerchiefs embroidered with silk twisted in their hair, and one of them wore a green satin night-cap.

Some of the women were very pretty. They were as scantily attired as the men; and three holes were bored in their lips, from which tin rings hung down.

Vasco exchanged toys and cloths with these natives for copper and ivory. He observed, in some of the clothes worn by the chiefs, marks of ochre; which confirmed his opinion that ships from India had been there, and that he was on the right way to that wonderful land.

It was just before leaving the River of Good Signs that two mishaps occurred, one of which nearly deprived the fleet of its intrepid captain. Vasco da Gama was standing in a boat, alongside the "San Gabriel," talking to his brother Paulo. He was holding on to the chains of the ship to steady himself, when, of a sudden, the boat was carried from under him by a strong current. For some moments he hung helpless upon the chains: his strength was fast giving out; when another boat shot up alongside, and he was pulled on board, and saved.

As the ships were sailing across the bar of the river, the "San Raphael" ran aground. At first it seemed inevitable that she must be lost; but fortunately, at the turn of the tide, she floated again, and proved to have received no injury.

Vasco da Gama, in bidding adieu to the River of Good Signs, left behind two of the criminals he had brought with him, to see what they could discover, and to be picked up again on the return voyage if they survived.

CHAPTER VII.

VASCO DA GAMA CAPTURES A MOOR, AND ARRIVES AT MOZAMBIQUE.

WELL satisfied that his voyage had so far been successful, and that, if he persevered, he would in no very long time reach India, Vasco da Gama still deemed it prudent to run along the African coast till he should reach some place where he could get trustworthy information where it would be best to strike directly across the ocean.

The sailors had given over all thoughts of turning back, and went to their work happily and with a will. The pilot of the "San Raphael" begged to be allowed to once more guide the ship, and was restored to his post. As for the criminals, they had lost all influence over the crews by their failure, and were disposed to be obedient and submissive. One sunny morning the ships were running along under a fair wind, making good speed, and showing by their steady motion that the repairs had been thorough.

Vasco da Gama was on the deck of the "San Raphael," gazing curiously at the coast, and chatting with his officers.

Of a sudden the pilot cried out, "A sail ahead!"

The captain could scarcely believe his ears. Why should there be a sail on these distant waters? So far, the savages they had found were only provided with rude canoes and oars. Had they already reached a region where the art of navigation was known?

Vasco da Gama hastened to the pilot's side; and there, sure enough, in the hazy distance, a boat with a sail could be distinctly seen skimming the smooth waters.

Vasco at once gave the order to bear down with all speed upon the sail. But now they had evidently been observed from the boat; for, by a sudden tack, it made off to the sea; and, after a long chase, the sail was lost sight of in the falling darkness. Vasco, though chagrined at failing to overhaul it, was consoled by the thought that the sail indicated the vicinity of a navigating people.

The next day, as the ships continued to skirt the shore, one of the sailors spied a rocky point stretching out into the sea; and off this point was anchored a peculiar sort of coastwise vessel, called a "zambuk." Just beyond the point, a large creek flowed down from the hills behind.

The ships had scarcely got opposite the point, when a canoe was seen leaving the zambuk, and making leisurely for the shore. There was no time to be lost. Vasco ordered some of his men to take a boat, and go in pursuit of the canoe. In a twinkling they were on the waves, and were rowing lustily towards the shore.

It was not long before the craft that was being pursued caught sight of the pursuers. The sailors perceived that it contained seven men. The Portuguese rapidly gained upon the canoe, and in a few moments were but a rod or two behind it.

Seeing this, six of the men in the boat, in their terror, plunged into the sea, and swam vigorously towards the shore, leaving their companion in the lurch, sitting helplessly alone in the canoe.

When the Portuguese came alongside, they

found that the man who had thus been abruptly left behind was not a Negro, nor a Caffre, but a Moor.

His complexion was cream-color, and his hair straight. He wore a white shirt, with a silk band around the waist. Over his shoulders was thrown a short cloak of colored cloth; and on his head he wore a round turban, made of wrappings of colored silk sewed with gold thread. From his ears hung a pair of small gold rings.

The Moor had sat still in the canoe simply because he could not swim. When the Portuguese seized him, and put him into their boat, his teeth chattered, and his frame trembled from excessive fright; but on the way back to the ships he became more composed.

The Portuguese went to the zambuk and searched it, but found nothing worth bringing away. They then carried their prisoner to the "San Raphael," and presented him to Vasco da Gama.

After a while the Moor recovered from his fright, and gave Vasco to understand by signs that he was the agent of a great Moorish merchant, and that he was about to embark a cargo of merchandise on board the zambuk. An African slave on the "San Raphael" spoke to him in Arabic, of which, however, he understood only a few words; explaining by signs, however, that, farther on, there were people who spoke that language.

Vasco da Gama treated the Moor rather as if he were a guest than a prisoner. He caused a long red robe to be brought and put on him; and he proffered him some cakes, olives, and wine. The Moor ate heartily of all that was set before him; but the wine he could not be prevailed on to touch.

Davane — this turned out to be the Moor's name — gradually became confident and at his ease; and the more Vasco da Gama saw of him, the more he was convinced that his prisoner was an unusually intelligent and honest man. He took him below, and showed him the spices he had brought as samples of what he wished to obtain; whereat Davane made him understand that he himself was a broker, and could put him in the way of some profitable commerce.

The Moor was soon able to give Vasco da Gama a convincing proof of his good faith. One day, as the ships were sailing along the coast, he eagerly pointed out some shoals and banks ahead, making signs that the pilots should go around, and thus avoid the danger of being stranded on them. These proved to be the Shoals of Sofala. The river of that name was passed in the night, and was not seen by the Portuguese; although the good Moor tried hard to tell them of it by pointing and imitating the flowing of a stream.

A day or two afterwards, another sail made its appearance at a little distance off. This time Vasco da Gama resolved that he would not be outsailed. The "San Raphael" edged out to sea, and the vessel was soon overhauled.

To the surprise of the Portuguese, the occupants of the zambuk — for such it proved to be — made no attempt to escape, but welcomed the sailors who were sent out in a boat to board her. Two Caffres willingly consented to return to the "San Raphael" with them; and, as soon as they appeared on deck, the Moor Davane, who seemed to recognize them at once, joyfully cried out that they were Caffres of Mozambique.

It happened that on board Paulo da Gama's ship was a Caffre from Guinea. He was at once sent for, and, to Vasco's delight, was found to be able to talk with the others. From them he learned that the zambuk, which was now lying quietly by awaiting their return, was laden with guano, of which some islands not far off contained an abundance; and that they were going to carry it to Cambay, where it was used in dyeing cloths.

Davane found that he, too, could communicate a little with the Caffres, and told Vasco da Gama what he learned from them. It appeared that some distance ahead was a large town, which carried on an active trade in all sorts of goods; that they were on the way to Cambay, which was a great kingdom and a rich country, especially in drugs and spices. Davane advised Vasco to keep a sharp lookout on the zambuk, and to make the Caffres guide the ships through the numerous shoals in this region. Vasco accordingly told the Caffres to return to their vessel, and keep on ahead with it, so as to show, by lanterns with which he provided them, when they were approaching the shoals in the night.

Meanwhile the captain manifested his gratitude to Davane, regaling him with the best there was on board, and assuring him that he should be bountifully rewarded for his services and fidelity.

It was towards the end of March that the ships, following always in the wake of the zambuk, entered the channel which runs between the large Island of Madagascar and the African coast. Here they began to come upon numerous small islands dotting the sea. Some of them had many trees; others were quite bare and sandy.

One evening Vasco da Gama descried four islands, two of them lying in close to the shore, and the others farther out in the sea. Scarcely had these appeared, when from one of the islands near the shore he perceived several canoes putting out, and rowing towards him.

When the canoes came near the "San Raphael," their occupants were seen to be very dark, but not as black as negroes. They wore handkerchiefs of various colors, some being wrought with gold-thread, wound around their heads, and coats of striped cotton, girdled at the knees; and Vasco was not sorry to observe that they were armed with swords and daggers, which showed that they had traded with civilized peoples.

These men, who proved to be Moors, came confidently on deck, as if they had found old friends. Viands and wine were set before them by Vasco's command, which they ate and drank without hesitation, and with great gusto.

Through the Moor Davane, who acted as an interpreter, and seemed rejoiced to see these people, Vasco was gratified to learn from his visitors that the island on which they lived was called Mozambique, where there was a large and flourishing town, which traded for silver, linen, pepper, ginger, pearls, and rubies, with the Moors of India.

Here then, at last, he had reached a place where he could doubtless procure definite information as to the distance they were from India, and the way to reach it. It now seemed as if the glorious end of his long and weary journey was about to be attained.

The Moors made the most eager professions of friendship, and offered to pilot the ships into the harbor of Mozambique. This offer Vasco da Gama accepted; and the canoes led the way, the Portuguese ships and the zambuk following in their wake.

The large sails were taken in, and the vessels soon floated into the deep and well-sheltered harbor under their foresails and mizzens.

The sight which now presented itself to Vasco and his men filled them with surprise and curiosity. They could plainly discern scattered over the island, which was beautiful in hilly verdure and luxuriant in foliage, the low but neat-looking houses, thatched with straw, of the native merchants.

Lying at anchor in the harbor, at a little distance off, were the strange-looking ships in which the Moors of Mozambique carried their goods to Sofala, and even perhaps to India itself, and brought back the silks, jewels, and precious spices of the East.

Vasco noticed that these ships had no decks at all; and that, instead of being fastened with nails, their planks were held together with thick cords, which he afterwards learned were made from the fibres of cocoanut-rinds. The sails, moreover, — great flabby-looking things, — were mats woven with palm-leaves. He was told that the Moorish pilots in these vessels actually used compasses made in Genoa, and had quadrants and even sea-charts to aid them in directing their courses across the ocean.

All along the shore were gathered crowds of

men, women, and children, many of them decked out in silk and silver ornaments, eagerly watching the strange ships, and pointing them out to each other.

Vasco sent on shore the Caffres whom he had compelled to come with him in the zambuk; and these soon returned, bringing with them some cocoanuts and two hens, which the Moors had sent as a proof of good will. The Caffres were sent back with some biscuit and cake, which they distributed to the people on the beach, who seemed to relish them very much.

Finding that the Moor Davane understood the natives of Mozambique, Vasco thought it well that he, too, should visit the village. Accordingly, Coello took him in a boat; and, when they got into shallow water, Davane nimbly jumped out, and waded ashore.

He was gone a long time; and Vasco began to fear that Davane had met with foul play, or had, after all, proved false. After some hours, however, he returned safe and sound to the "San Raphael," and lost no time in acquainting Vasco da Gama with what had befallen him on the island.

As soon as he got ashore the people surrounded him, and began to ask him all sorts of questions. Where did these ships come from? Where were they going to? Who were the white people in them?

Replying as best he could, Davane was escorted to the house of the sheik, or governor, who, it seemed, ruled in Mozambique in the name of the King of Quiloa. The sheik received him cordially; and Davane told him who the Portuguese were, and whither they were going.

Then the sheik in turn informed Davane that almost all the people in Mozambique were Moors, and traded a great deal, not only in spices and stuffs, but in gold, ivory, and wax. He added, that he should like very much to visit the ships of the strangers; and, giving Davane some cocoanuts, chickens, figs, and mutton, bade him return and present them to the captain, and tell him the sheik would pay him a visit.

Vasco da Gama hastened to reciprocate the sheik's friendly advances. He sent Davane back to assure him that he would be most welcome whenever he chose to come on board; and that the Portuguese were anxious to secure his friendship, and trade with him, as they were wanderers from a far-off land. Meanwhile Vasco took good care to send some presents to the sheik, among them a red cap, some black beads, coral, brass basins, bells, and gowns.

When Davane gave these things with Vasco's messages to the swarthy potentate, he looked at them contemptuously, and, turning to the Moor, asked why the captain had not sent him some scarlet cloth.

Davane replied that there was none on board, and then cordially invited the sheik to visit the ships.

"Return to the captain," replied the sheik, "and tell him that I will come and visit him this afternoon."

Davane hurried back, and told Vasco what the sheik had said; and Vasco gave orders that preparations should be make forthwith to receive so important a personage in a manner befitting his rank and dignity.

CHAPTER VIII.

ADVENTURES AT MOZAMBIQUE.

THE sheik was as good as his word. Scarcely had Vasco da Gama finished his mid-day meal, when one of the sailors came running to him with the news that several boats were putting out from the shore, one of which contained some Moors in very handsome dresses.

The "San Raphael" had been gayly decked out to receive the noble guests. Flags and streamers fluttered from the masts and sails. A pretty tent, trimmed with ribbons of many colors, had been set up on deck; carpets had been spread, and chairs and benches had been arranged, for the occasion. Vasco had ordered all the sick and infirm men to stay below; while the rest of his men provided themselves with arms, lest the Moors should show signs of treachery.

Paulo da Gama and Nicolas Coello had joined their chief on the "San Raphael," and all three of the captains were dressed in rich velvet coats and plumed caps. They now took their places on the quarter-deck, and awaited the coming of the sheik. The canoes were fast approaching the ship; and soon Vasco was able to perceive that that which carried the sheik was really a raft, made of two boats lashed together, and a platform of planks laid over them, and provided with an awning of mats. Beneath this sat the sheik, on a low, round stool covered with rich silk. On the raft with the sheik were ten other Moors, evidently of high rank.

Just as the Moorish boats drew up alongside the "San Raphael," the trumpets sounded a loud welcome. Then the sailors aided the swarthy dignitary and his companions to ascend on board, where they were met and cordially saluted by Vasco and Paulo da Gama, who bowed low to the sheik. Paulo being the elder of the brothers, the sheik mistook him for the chief of the fleet. Taking Paulo's hand, he raised it to his breast in token of respect, and said something in a low voice which the captains could not understand.

Visit of the Sheik at Mozambique. Page 94.

The sheik was then conducted beneath the tent, where he was offered a chair covered with a handsome carpet. His attendants were provided with places on a long bench which had been placed near by. Vasco and Paulo sat on either side of their guest, and the Moor Davane stood just behind the chairs to act as interpreter; for, by this time, Davane had picked up enough Portuguese to converse a little with Vasco and his men.

At first, nothing was said; the sheik looking around very curiously and deliberately, and taking note of every thing on board, as if he had never seen the like of the "San Raphael" before. Meanwhile the Portuguese were able to observe him and his companions at their leisure.

The sheik was a tall, dark, slender man, of graceful form and presence, with large black eyes and black flowing beard. He wore a long jacket of plaited red Mecca velvet, and a blue cloak embroidered with gold and silver lace; loose white breeches which reached to his knees; a broad sash about his waist, in which glistened a silver-handled dagger. On his head rested a huge silk turban of various colors, ornamented with gold thread and lace; and on his feet were a pair of silken shoes. In his hand the sheik held a silver-mounted sword. As he sat under the tent, he looked a very magnificent personage indeed; and the Portuguese gathered around him, and gazed at him admiringly.

The noble Moors who had come with him were scarcely less splendid in their apparel and adornments. They were fine-looking men, with silk robes and bright-colored turbans. Some were quite fair, others were brown, and yet others nearly black. Attending the sheik were several musicians, who had ivory trumpets and other curious instruments with which to entertain the strangers.

After the sheik had taken a good look at the ship and its company, he began to speak in Arabic; and the Moor Davane slowly translated what he said to Vasco, and also what Vasco replied to the sheik. The following conversation took place: —

"I am very glad you have come to my port," said the sheik; "and all that I can do to aid you I will, for to see you gives me much pleasure. There are many things here that I have not seen before. Are you foreign merchants? And from what country are you? What brings you hither?"

"We are from a far country called Portugal," returned Vasco, "and are the subjects of one of the greatest kings in Christendom."

"I supposed you were Turks, from your being so fair; but it appears you are not."

"We have cargoes of merchandise which we wish to exchange for other articles, and are trying to find India; but alas! my lord, our pilots know not which way to steer to reach it."

"And if you do not find India," asked the sheik, smiling, "what will you do?"

"We shall go about the seas until we die; for we should fear to return to our king without having found that which we came to seek."

"Show me, then, specimens of the merchandise of which you are in search."

Vasco ordered some pepper, cinnamon, and ginger to be brought and shown to him.

On seeing these spices the sheik turned round to his companions, and laughed and nodded, saying, —

"Oh! you may find plenty of these in this region, and I will give you pilots who will carry you where you can get as much as you please. But what have you brought to exchange for them ?"

"We have gold and silver."

"Well, with gold and silver you may buy any thing the world over. Pray, sir, will you not have your men blow on those things again ?"

The sheik pointed to the trumpets, which were sounded as he wished; whereat he seemed very much pleased, bending forward to listen to them.

"Now," he went on, "I wish you would show me your bows and arrows, and the books of your law."

Some cross-bows and armor were brought, and were examined by the Moor with the greatest curiosity and surprise.

"We have no books of the law," said Vasco, "as they are not needed at sea." Vasco now thought it his turn to ask questions, and inquired of the sheik how far it was from Mozambique to India; to which the latter replied, "About nine hundred leagues."

"And where is the land of the famous Prester John ?"

"Oh! it is far away from here, in the inland country," returned the sheik, pointing northward.

Vasco ordered that the best meats and wines the ship afforded should be set before his guests, who feasted upon the viands with hungry eagerness, and grew very merry and talkative over the wine.

It was sundown before the Moors, appearing much pleased with all they had seen and heard on board the "San Raphael," embarked again in their boats, and returned to the island. As the sheik went away with many friendly signs and expressions, he promised that he would send Vasco two pilots, who would conduct him safely to his destination.

The next day Vasco da Gama sent the Moor Davane on shore with some presents for the sheik. Among them were some pieces of satin cloth, two caps, five Flemish knives of fine temper, and a present of money for the pilots whom the sheik had promised him. He told Davane to buy some cows and sheep, and such other provisions as he could find.

Davane ere long returned with the two pilots,

and reported that all the food he could find was some corn, but that they could procure sheep and cows farther along the coast. The pilots were comfortably lodged in the forecastle, and were treated with every kindness by the Portuguese. Little did Vasco suspect with what treachery he was to be repaid for his hospitality.

Davane again went on shore to complete his purchases; and now the sheik took him apart in his house, and asked him many questions about Vasco da Gama and the ships. How many men were there? Were they all well? or were some of them sick? What kind of arms had they? How much merchandise and gold and silver were there on board? Davane replied that on the "San Raphael" there were about sixty men-at-arms, whose weapons were swords and lances; that the Portuguese were Christians, but good men and strong, and friendly to those that were friendly to them; that there were some who were sick; and that they had cross-bows and cannon. The more the sheik questioned him, the more did Davane suspect that his object in doing so was not an honest one.

"Go back to the captain," said the sheik, "and

invite him to come on shore and dine with me; and ask him to send his sick here, that they may be cared for."

As the faithful Davane rowed back to the "San Raphael" he resolved to impart his suspicions to Vasco da Gama, and to warn him not to accept the sheik's insidious invitation; for which Vasco warmly thanked him.

Davane's surmises soon proved only too true. The sheik and his companions, when they learned that the Portuguese were not Turks, as they had supposed, but were Christians, became secretly hostile to them; and, their cupidity having been aroused by the sight of the rich goods and coins which Vasco had displayed, they resolved at the same time to obtain them, and to destroy the heretic strangers.

There were four Moorish ships at anchor in the harbor, which the sheik ordered to be in readiness to attack the Portuguese ships. He called together the Moors in the town, and told them his purpose, and to prepare to make an attack. Vasco da Gama was happily forewarned by his good friend Davane; but not wishing to create enemies along the coast, lest he should get a bad reputation in those regions, he would have sailed away at once, had it not been necessary to take in fresh water for the ships.

How was this to be done? They did not know where there were streams to get water from; and they were now certain, that, if they approached the shore, they would be savagely attacked.

Vasco thought he would first try to propitiate the sheik; and, that failing, he would send a boat well armed on the perilous errand of seeking for water.

Davane was accordingly sent a third time on shore, and was welcomed by the sheik with a great show of pretended friendship. He told him that Vasco da Gama could not disembark in any country except that to which King Manuel had sent him, and so could not accept his invitation to dine; and begged the sheik to tell him where water could best be procured. This the sheik pretended to do; pointing out a place, however, where the Portuguese could be easily attacked by his Moors. Davane then returned to the ship with this new proof of the sheik's evil designs.

It now only remained to send out a boat, filled with well-armed men, in search of a stream. The risk was great; but water, if possible, must be obtained.

A large boat was soon lowered, and Nicolas Coello was put in command of it. He carried with him two cannon, ten sailors, and twelve men with cross-bows; and one of the Moorish pilots, whom the sheik had sent on board, was ordered to accompany the expedition, and guide the boat to a convenient creek. A sharp watch was kept on him to see that he did not betray them, or make signals to the shore.

It was midnight when the boat set out on its errand. It was safer to go under the cover of the darkness; and, besides, they had to take advantage of the high tide, lest they should run aground at the mouths of the creeks. Before long, it became evident that the Moorish pilot was trying to play them false. He directed them first to one place, and then to another, pretending to point out a stream where water could be got; and so long a time was thus occupied, that, before Coello knew it, the tide had receded, and he was in great danger of being stuck on the beach. This was, no doubt, what the pilot desired.

The men rowed desperately, and at last succeeded in getting out into the bay again. Then they cried out, angrily, that the treacherous pilot should be killed on the spot. Coello himself was sorely tempted to make an end of him; but reflecting that Vasco da Gama would perhaps wish to have him hung on the deck, so that the people on shore might see how traitors were treated, he forbore.

Daylight had now come, and the boat was crossing the bay. At a favorable moment, and before the men could prevent him, the Moorish pilot suddenly leaped overboard. He dived deep into the sea, and it was some minutes before the Portuguese caught sight of him again. He swam under water a long distance, and came up, too far away to be reached by the cross-bows, striking out vigorously toward the shore.

Coello ordered the men to row after him, but presently was forced to turn back again, as the shore was now crowded with enraged Moors, who shot arrows, and threw stones from slings, at his little company, endangering the lives of all.

The boat went back to the "San Raphael." And now Vasco da Gama had to decide whether he should attack the town, or go quietly away.

On the one hand, he was angry at the perfidy of the sheik and the pilot, and was sure that he could easily destroy the place with his cannon, if he chose: on the other, he did not wish it to be reported along the coast that the Portuguese had come to fight and plunder.

Peaceful counsels at last prevailed. Vasco determined to proceed on the voyage, the other Moorish pilot having been put in irons. Just as they were making sail, however, Vasco saw a boat push out from the island, containing four Caffres and a Moor. They had a white cloth fastened at the end of a pole, which they flourished as a flag of truce. Vasco caused the "San Raphael" to heave to, and the Moor came on board. He told the captain, through Davane, that the sheik was astonished at the Portuguese for trying to kill his pilot, and at their going away so abruptly; adding, that, if any of his people had ill treated them, he would see to it that the offenders were punished. Upon this, Vasco da Gama wished to send Davane back to Mozambique with a friendly message; but Davane begged that he might not be sent, for he was afraid that the sheik would kill him.

So the captain ordered one of the convicts whom he had brought with him to go back with the Caffres, and to remain at Mozambique till he returned from India.

This convict, whose name was Joan Machado, was very unwilling to trust himself thus among enemies; but Vasco was obdurate, and Machado was forced to get into the canoe.

He was ordered to tell the sheik that the Moorish pilot had treacherously failed to guide the boat to a place where water could be obtained; and that, as the sheik had not treated the Portuguese with sincerity, they were going away without bidding him adieu.

The little fleet now once more weighed anchor, and put off to sea, carrying several Moors who had fallen into the hands of the Portuguese. As she was sailing away, the "San Raphael" drifted upon a sand-bank, but was happily got off again by the exertions of the crews before the Moors could take advantage of the accident.

Before following Vasco on his voyage, we may briefly relate what afterward befell the convict, Joan Machado, who was sent so unceremoniously back to Mozambique. The sheik, instead of ordering him away to be beheaded, treated him well, and, as Joan knew a little Arabic, often talked with him. Thus Joan got into his good graces, and was allowed to remain in peace at Mozambique as long as he pleased.

It happened, that, when the "San Raphael" ran aground, another convict, named Rodriguez, a friend of Machado's, availed himself of the confusion to escape from the ship, and swam ashore. He soon joined Machado at the sheik's house, and both Machado and the sheik were delighted to see him.

After being in Mozambique for some time, poor Rodriguez died; and his faithful friend, procuring the consent of the sheik, buried him at the end of the island, and put a rude cross over the grave.

Joan Machado soon learned to talk glibly with the Moors; and being a fine-looking man, with pleasant manners and much intelligence, he soon won the friendship of the whole population as well as of the sheik.

He told them how great and powerful the King of Portugal was, and that he was resolved to send fleets to India until he conquered it: whereupon the sheik made up his mind that he would as soon as possible retrieve his error, and make friends with the Portuguese.

Machado travelled about from country to country along the coast, and finally made his way to India. He traded and grew rich, and was held in the highest esteem by the Moors among whom he lived.

CHAPTER IX.

VASCO DA GAMA ARRIVES AT MOMBAZA.

THE wind did not at first serve the caravels. After going a league from Mozambique, they cast anchor, and the Portuguese disembarked upon a small and uninhabited island. Here Vasco da Gama caused the priests to set up an altar, and say mass; while the crews stood around and listened to the solemn service of thanks with uncovered heads. Then the priests heard the men confess; and on the following day, which was Sunday, the sacrament was administered.

A favorable breeze springing up, Vasco da Gama pursued his voyage along the coast. He was not a little perplexed to decide whether he had best keep close to the shore, or strike out boldly across the ocean towards India. From the Moorish pilot whom he questioned he could get but little information, and what little he got he could not believe.

This Moor, enraged because he had been put in irons, resolved to bring the fleet to ruin if he could. He told Vasco that some leagues farther on was the great city of Quiloa, which was inhabited half by Christians, and half by Moors. It was quite true that the ships were going towards Quiloa; but there were no Christians there at all. The pilot's object was to lure Vasco into the harbor of Quiloa, raise the alarm among the Moors there, and so wreak vengeance on the Portuguese.

Davane, always awake to the dangers of the voyage, and entirely devoted to Vasco, warned him not to put in at Quiloa, but to distrust the pilot in every thing.

Vasco then called the pilot to him, and sternly told him that if any mishap occurred to the ships, or if they ran upon shoals, he would have both his eyes put out.

The fleet passed Quiloa in the night, driven on by the currents; and, a strong gale coming on, the ships were tossed about, and were with difficulty kept on their course. As they were making the best headway they could through the gale, Paulo da Gama's ship, very early one morning, ran suddenly aground upon a sand-bank, six miles out from the coast. Paulo hastened to make a signal to his brother, who lost no time in coming to his assistance.

Vasco was glad to see that the tide was low, and was confident that when it rose again the ship would probably float. At daylight the "San Gabriel" lay quite dry upon the bank; and, while this was the state of affairs, some Moors came unexpectedly out to the ships in a canoe, bringing with them a quantity of sweet oranges, which the Portuguese enjoyed very much. These Moors assured Vasco that the ship was in no danger, for at flood-tide she would easily float off again. This proved to be the case; and the fleet continued on its journey, carrying away several of the Moors, who begged to go with the Portuguese to Mombaza.

It was late in April when the caravels, progressing to the north-east, arrived off the island and town of Mombaza. Vasco perceived that this town stood picturesquely on the summit and sides of a rocky hill; and that many of the houses were well built, and of stone. It seemed a lovely place: for on the hills round about could be discerned orchards of pomegranates, figs, oranges, lemons, and citrons; while, in the pastures, fat cattle and sheep were lazily browsing in the sun.

Vasco saw that there was a good harbor, but that it could only be approached by passing some shoals; and this, as well as the doubt whether he would be well received by the potentate and people of Mombaza, caused him to anchor at some little distance off the island.

From the Moors who were on board the "San Gabriel," however, he learned a great deal about the town. They told him that the harbor was excellent, and that there was an active trade between Mombaza and the coast, mainly in honey, wax, and ivory. The inhabitants were Moors,—some very fair-skinned, and others swarthy; and they dressed richly, especially the women, who wore costly silks. As for the houses, they were as handsome within as on the outside, being plastered, and replete with ornaments; while the streets presented a wide and pleasant aspect. The town had plenty of provisions, they added, especially rice and millet. The Moors told him, moreover, that the town was ruled over by an independent king of its own; and they added, falsely, that many Christians lived there.

All this made Vasco da Gama anxious to communicate with Mombaza, to make friends with the king, trade with him if possible, and find out the best route thence to that India which he more and more longed to behold.

Unhappily, he was destined here to meet with the same craft and treachery which had so often marked his intercourse with the dwellers along the African coast. The King of Mombaza had already learned from the perfidious Sheik of Mozambique, who had sent forward some swift coastwise vessels, that the Portuguese were Christians; and he had resolved to serve them an ill turn as soon as they reached his port. To do this, he used the same hypocrisy which the sheik had already done.

No sooner were the ships at anchor than the king sent out some boats laden with an abundance of good things, — chickens, sheep, sugar-canes, lemons, citrons, and large, sweet oranges, that tasted deliciously. The sick were delighted to get these luxuries, which wonderfully revived their health and spirits.

Vasco distrusted the accounts of his Moors, and took every precaution to avoid a surprise. Yet it might be that what they said was true; and he was anxious, if possible, to conciliate the king. He was ignorant of the warning the king had received from the sheik, and thought it at least possible that there might be Christians, who would surely be friends, living at Mombaza.

When he received this generous present of provisions, therefore, he ordered the flags to be hoisted on the masts, and the trumpets to be sounded, in token that he wished to be friendly with the king.

A venerable-looking Moor, richly clad, and with a long, flowing white beard, now came on board with a message from his royal master. He told Vasco that the king welcomed him to Mombaza, and would like to come on board the "San Raphael;" and that the captain was quite at liberty to enter the harbor, and to visit the town. At the same time, the king sent two pilots to conduct the ships safely by the bar into port.

Vasco sent the old Moor back with an amicable

message; but scarcely had he departed when a large boat came out from the island, with a hundred Moors in it armed to the teeth. On reaching the "San Raphael," all these men wished to go on board at once: but Vasco only permitted them to go four at a time, and without their arms; at the same time explaining to them that the Portuguese were strangers, and had learned by experience to be suspicious. The Moors answered that they only came armed because that was the invariable custom of their country, and readily accepted the cakes and wine which Vasco caused to be distributed among them. They told him how glad the king was that he had come, and that the king would not only visit him, but would load his ships with spices; adding, that it was true that there were many Christians living in Mombaza.

Nothing could be more cunning, as will presently appear, than the way in which the King of Mombaza tried to calm Vasco's suspicions, that he might fall into the trap set for him.

The next morning some Moors, very fair in complexion, came off to the ships. They asserted that they were Christians; and among the many messages which they brought from the king was a request that some of the Portuguese should go ashore and visit the city, and see its Christian inhabitants. Vasco da Gama once more had recourse to the convicts whom he had brought with him to be sent on dangerous errands. Two of these he ordered to return with the white Moors, which they accordingly did.

They were met, on landing, by crowds of finely-dressed people, men and women, who looked at them with much curiosity, and followed them to the royal palace. Here the convicts were conducted through three doors, each of which was guarded by a Moorish sentinel; and in a small apartment, at the farther end of the palace, they found the king himself. He received them with much courtesy, and calling the old white-bearded Moor whom he had first sent to Vasco, and who seemed to be a sort of marshal or major-domo, told him to conduct the strangers through the town, and to let them take whatever caught their fancy without any charge.

As the two convicts passed through the streets, which were really spacious and well built, they saw here and there men lying in irons. These they conjectured to be Christians, but dared or could not ask.

Pretty soon they reached a large, rather imposing house, which they were invited to enter. At the threshold they were met by several fine-looking, fair-skinned, well-dressed men, who led the way to a room within. These assured the convicts that they were Christians, and, to prove it, brought out some beads with crosses hanging to them, which they put to their eyes, and reverently kissed. They also produced a picture representing the Holy Ghost, before which they fell upon their knees.

These pretended Christians regaled the convicts with rice-cakes, butter, honey, and fruit, and begged that they would stay over night at their house; but the old Moor who acted as guide forbade this, and carried the convicts back to the palace, where they slept.

The next morning the king took pains to show them his plentiful stores of spices, ginger, pepper, and cloves, and told them that he had besides an abundance of gold, silver, amber, wax, and ivory, which he would sell very cheaply to the Portuguese.

One of the convicts now returned to the "San Raphael," and narrated to Vasco da Gama what had passed. The captain was somewhat re-assured to see him come back safely, and still more so at the mild and friendly conduct of the Moors, who continued to come to the ships with presents, and messages of good will. The other convict, as Vasco had commanded, remained at Mombaza.

The king having sent two pilots on board, Vasco da Gama resolved to venture into the harbor. If worst came to worst, he had his sturdy crossbow-men and his cannon to defend him from an attack; and he little doubted that he could make the Moors rue any attempt at treachery they might make.

The next morning the pilots declared that the tide was rising, and that now was the time to cross the sandy bar which lay between the ships and the harbor. The Portuguese pilots exclaimed angrily against this, and pointed out to the captain that the tide was not a quarter full. To this the Mombaza men replied that at full tide the water ran too strong for the ships.

Vasco ordered the anchors to be weighed. The

old Moor who had come out with some armed men led the way with his boat. And now a curious thing happened. The "San Raphael" could not be brought round with her prow towards the channel, despite every exertion of the sailors, but, instead, drifted straight upon the bank.

"Let the anchor fall, and strike the sails!" shouted Vasco; and his order was echoed by his brother on the other ship, which was close by.

The next thing they knew, the "San Raphael" stuck by her stern upon the bar. The old Moor, whose real purpose was to get the ships aground, thought he had succeeded, and rowed hastily away to the shore. At the same time, one of the Mombaza pilots seized a moment of confusion to leap into the sea, and swim lustily for the Moorish canoes; one of which soon picked him up, and carried him safely to the island.

Before the other Mombaza pilot could follow his comrade's example, he was seized. And now Vasco da Gama began to suspect that the Moors he had brought from Mozambique had been plotting with those of Mombaza to destroy the ships.

He ordered them to be brought on deck, and questioned them. As they refused to reply, he had some boiling hot grease brought, and dropped upon their bare backs. Writhing with the torture, they at last cried out that they would reveal every thing. They then confessed that they were in league with the Moors of Mombaza; and that the king had planned to get the ships upon the banks, to kill all the Portuguese, and to plunder the caravels.

There was still another Moor on board, who, Vasco thought, might be in the plot. He was brought on deck, and his hands were tied together; but, before he could be put to the torture, he suddenly jumped overboard, and swam away with his legs, being, of course, unable to use his arms.

The next thing was to get the "San Raphael" off the bar. Fortunately, night soon came on, and the moon rose full and clear. With the turn of the tide Vasco found with joy that his ship floated off the sands. But a new obstacle to their departure now presented itself. One of the anchors which had been cast, stuck fast in the shallows, and the men worked all night to haul it up again.

While this work was going on, a number of

Moors came out in boats; and, before long, the sailors who were at work on the anchor, felt something tugging at the cable. At first, they thought this caused by a shoal of tunny-fish; but, on looking more closely, they caught some of the Moors, who had clambered up on the side, and were in the act of cutting the cable so that the ship might drift ashore. Before they could be reached by the boats of the "San Gabriel," however, these black rascals jumped into the sea, and swam off to their own canoes.

It would appear that they had at least succeeded in damaging the cable; for, while the men were trying to weigh the anchor, the cable broke, and they were forced to leave the anchor sticking in the bottom. This anchor was afterwards got out by the Moors, who placed it as a curiosity at the gate of the royal palace, where it was seen some years after by a Portuguese navigator named Don Francesco d'Almeida.

Still another danger menaced the ships. It was feared that the Moors of Mombaza, having failed to strand them on the shore, would set fire to them. A strict watch was therefore kept through the night, and cannon were placed in a position to rake the Moorish boats if they should come up.

Probably the Moors caught sight of the guns, and were afraid to venture; for morning came without any attack having been made, and almost as soon as it was light the caravels were once more speeding north-eastward along the African coast.

CHAPTER X.

SOJOURN AT MELINDA.

VASCO DA GAMA had hitherto met with nothing but craft and treachery from the inhabitants and princes who dwelt along the coast; and had begun to despair of finding any friendship or sincerity among them, or of procuring information upon which he might depend.

He was soon to find, however, both a king and a people who presented a most favorable contrast to those he had so far visited; who would welcome him, and treat him generously, and set him fairly on the way to India.

Meanwhile the voyage along the coast was not without incident. One afternoon he spied two zambuks running in to land. Bearing down upon them, he succeeded in capturing one: the other was a little too quick for him; for, running into a narrow inlet, it escaped.

Vasco found that the vessel he had taken was laden with ivory, and contained a large number of Moors. It was commanded by an old Moor named Dias, who, it seems, had a pretty young wife on board, whom he was taking home with him. There were four other women, who were attendants of the bride; and in the boat was also a large chest, which proved to be full of her jewels and a quantity of gold and silver coins.

Vasco resolved to take some of these Moors with him, among them the old captain and his wife: the rest he allowed to depart in the zambuk in peace. He tried to find among his prisoners a pilot to guide his ship; for the Mozambique pilot was still sternly kept in irons. But these Moors all declared that they could not pilot her, even though they should be put to the torture.

He managed, however, to get along very well without their aid. The weather was pleasant, and light west breezes wafted the ships along. In three nights and two days they reached Melinda, between fifty and sixty miles north-eastward from Mombaza; a town of which they had heard glowing accounts, and which Vasco was very anxious to see.

His expectations were more than realized. His ships were anchored in the roadstead, at some distance from the shore, because there seemed to be no good harbor; but, from the quarter-deck where the intrepid captain stood, he could plainly see, not only the town, but the country round about it.

He was amazed at the imposing spectacle which met his eyes. At the edge of the water rose a ridge, or reef of rocks, which formed a natural pier; but the waves beat so violently against this reef, that it was unsafe for the ships to venture close to it.

Beyond the reef appeared the town, or, as it better deserved to be called, the city, standing upon a broad, open, and fertile plain. Vasco could see that it was a large and flourishing place, adorned by noble stone buildings two or three stories high, with windows and terraced roofs. The city was surrounded by walls; and here and there a mosque was seen, its dome rising above the neighboring edifices. The suburbs of Melinda were really beautiful. Stretching off over the hills, beyond the walls, were groves of graceful palm-trees, gardens full of the most brilliant flowers, and orchards of oranges, lemons, and other tropical fruits. Everywhere the grass was of the brightest, richest green; and the landscape in every direction was fair and lovely.

In the roadstead off the town lay a number of strange-looking vessels, which Vasco rightly guessed to be Moorish traders, that ran between Melinda and various points on the coast, and also to the more remote ports of Asia.

The Portuguese were delighted to find themselves near a city which they declared to be scarcely inferior to Lisbon itself in size and civilized aspect; and Vasco da Gama caused prayers of thanksgiving for their safe arrival to be offered up by the priests on the decks. He felt confident, that, at Melinda, he would find pilots to conduct him to India; and he was impatient to open communication with the ruler of the city.

At first, no notice seemed to be taken of his arrival. No boats came out to visit the ships, nor was there any unusual stir on shore. It appeared afterwards that the people of Melinda feared the Portuguese, and suspected they had come rather as marauders than for any peaceful purpose.

While Vasco was considering what he should

do, the old Moor Dias, whom he had taken in the zambuk, and who was anxious to get away home again with his young wife, came up and spoke to the captain.

"Sir," he said, "I see four Christian ships from the Indies lying at anchor in the roadstead; and I know that there are many Christian traders in Melinda. If you will put me ashore, I will engage to get you some Christian pilots as my ransom; hoping that, in your goodness, you will then let me depart with my wife."

Vasco resolved to trust the old Moor; and, anchoring his ship somewhat nearer the coast, he caused Dias to be put ashore on a ledge opposite the city. No sooner was he left alone than a boat came from Melinda to fetch him.

He was at once conducted to the presence of the king, who proved to be the most powerful monarch on the coast, and who lived in a palace in which a European prince might not have been ashamed to dwell. Dias without ado told the king whence the ships came, and what their errand was at so great a distance from home. He told him how badly the Portuguese had been treated at Mozambique and Mombaza, and how they had generously refrained from avenging the treachery of the potentates of those places.

The King of Melinda seemed to lend a favorable ear to Dias's story, and forthwith sent a boat laden with fruits and provisions to the "San Raphael" as a token of good will. At the same time he ordered flags to be displayed from the walls of the city, and Vasco returned the compliment by raising standards and streamers on his masts. The king sent a message to the captain, inviting him to come within the port.

Vasco da Gama then despatched the Moor Davane, in whom he most trusted, to thank the king, and to report to him whether it appeared that the king was sincere in his advances.

Davane arrayed himself in a long red robe, and went ashore. He delivered his messages, and told his Majesty, that, when the pilot thought it safe, the ships would enter the port. The king took a fancy to Davane, and sat a long time talking with him. Then he summoned a council of his nobles and advisers, and asked them whether he should welcome the strangers, and whether it was wise to admit them within the port.

These wise men advised him with one accord

to do so: for the Portuguese seemed good men; and, if they turned out to be not so, they could be driven away by the royal forces.

Davane remained in the palace over night, and was regaled with sweet oranges and other delicacies. The next morning he was rowed off to the ship again, in company with the chief priest of the mosque, a man of great dignity and consequence, who was sent by the king as his envoy to Vasco da Gama. The boat also carried a generous present of sheep, fowls, oranges, sugar-canes, and vegetables, for the Portuguese.

The chief priest was cordially greeted by Vasco da Gama. He was invited to sit in a chair on deck; and preserves were brought to him in a silver basin, with a napkin, the latter being a token of hearty welcome.

Meanwhile Davane entertained Vasco with what he had seen at Melinda. He said that the houses were really fine, and the streets spacious and pleasant. The natives were very dark, but tall and well made, with long curly hair. There were a great many foreign merchants in the city, both Moors and Arabs. The better class of these bore themselves with grave dignity, and had polished manners. They were naked down to the waist, below which they wore silk or fine cotton skirts; while on their heads were wound large turbans of many colors, embroidered with silk and gold. At their girdles they wore daggers and swords with richly wrought handles and silk tassels; and many of them, being fond of archery, carried also bows and arrows. It appeared, curiously enough, that these Arabs were all left-handed. They prided themselves on their horsemanship.

Davane saw in the streets bazaars filled not only with fruit and grain, but articles made of gold, and a great deal of ivory, wax, pitch, and ambergris; and he learned that the Hindoo merchants received these for copper, quicksilver, and cotton cloth. He saw many merchants, who, he was told, were Christians. He described the king as a fine-looking old man, with a benignant face, gorgeously dressed, living in great state and ceremony, and attended by a large retinue of courtiers and servants.

Vasco da Gama, highly pleased with the friendly advances of the king, thought he would show his gratitude by saluting the city with his artillery. He ordered all the cannon on both ships to be fired off at the same moment; and, as the balls went skimming and whizzing over the water, the town felt the concussion, and the din caused not a little amazement and trepidation among the people. They were soon re-assured, however, and gathered in crowds on the shore to hear the trumpets sounded, as Vasco ordered they should be. The chief priest was now invited to return to the king with courteous messages; but, for some reason, he hesitated to go. Vasco could not understand this, and, calling Davane, asked what it meant.

"He means," said Davane, "that he has been ordered to stay on board as a hostage for the old Moor Dias, who is still with the king."

But Vasco wished to show the king that he confided in his offers of friendship, and so sent the chief priest away, presenting him with a string of corals. He also sent the king a hat, and some scarfs, basins, and bells, and told the priest what things he wished to be sent on board from the town. In the mean time the king closely questioned the Moor Dias as to how he came upon the Portuguese ship, and what kind of men he found the strangers to be.

"Sir," returned Dias, "the Christians on board the ships are good men. They took me and my wife and companions prisoners; but they have not harmed any of us, nor have they taken away our money and jewels. I pray you, sir, to entreat them to set us free, that I may return with my young wife to my own country."

The king readily promised that he would secure their release if possible; and no sooner had he made the request than Vasco granted it, sending ashore Dias's chest and other property untouched. The young wife was also allowed to rejoin her husband, and the rest of his company were restored to him.

On seeing them, and hearing that he was once more at liberty, old Dias exclaimed to the sailors, —

"The God of heaven requite you well, and restore you to your country in health and safety!"

To which the men shouted, "Amen, amen!"

Dias with his company then went before the king, thanked him with tears in their eyes, kissed his feet, and hastened away rejoicing.

The next day was an eventful one to the Portuguese, for then they looked upon men holding their own Christian faith for the first time since, a long and weary year before, they had sailed out of Lisbon harbor.

Vasco, in the morning, ventured to move his ships up nearer the city; and thus found himself in close proximity to the four Christian trading-vessels which the Moor Dias had pointed out to him.

No sooner did these Christian merchants see the "San Raphael" and the "San Gabriel" near them than a number of them came off to pay a visit to the strangers.

Vasco da Gama happened to be with his brother Paulo on the "San Gabriel:" so the visitors were invited to come on board that ship.

When they appeared on deck, Vasco was struck with their courteous bearing and intelligent faces. They were swarthy (but less so than the Moors he had been meeting along the coast), tall, and finely-proportioned, with long beards, and long hair, which was plaited up under their spacious turbans. They were dressed in cotton gowns of various colors, which extended nearly to their feet: about their waists they wore girdles, from which hung long swords.

Vasco da Gama welcomed his guests with the

refined grace which was natural to him; but he had been deceived so many times, that he resolved to try and find out whether these men were really Christians or not.

Bringing out a picture of the Virgin, who was represented as weeping, while a group of the apostles stood around her, he showed it to them without saying a word.

As soon as they saw it, they knelt down on the deck of one accord, and lifted their hands reverently towards the picture. Then they bowed their heads, and remained for several moments silently praying.

Vasco hastened to embrace them, and, inviting them to sit, held a long conversation with them through an interpreter. They told him that they were from India, and gave him a glowing account of that country; and Vasco was rejoiced to hear that India might be reached, without great difficulty, from Melinda.

On the following day the king sent word that he intended to come and visit the Portuguese, unless Vasco da Gama would come on shore.

The brothers Vasco and Paulo consulted together whether it was best to venture on land;

and Vasco insisted, that, if either of them risked the danger of doing so, he, as the younger, should be the one. But they were not as yet fully convinced of the king's good faith; and they finally resolved to send him word that King Manuel had forbidden them to land in foreign countries, but that they would come near the shore in their boats to see him. At the same time, to soften their refusal, they sent the king some red cloth, satin, and a large, beautifully-gilded Flemish mirror.

It was not long before the king showed them that he was not offended; for about nightfall another message arrived from him, that he would be glad to welcome the captains as soon as they chose to come.

CHAPTER XI.

VASCO VISITS THE KING OF MELINDA.

BEFORE fulfilling his promise to trust himself and his brother Paulo near the shore, Vasco da Gama thought it best to send the other captain, Coello, to Melinda, with the Moor Davane, to have an interview with the king, and see if he were really sincere.

Accordingly, the next day, Coello and Davane went off in a boat, and landed on a quay not far from the royal palace. Coello was very handsomely dressed; and so eager was the curiosity of the inhabitants to see him, and so closely did they press around him, that the king's guard were forced to resort to blows to keep them at a respectful distance.

Coello and the Moor were at once conducted within the palace, and ushered into the royal

Vasco Visits the King of Melinda. Page 137.

presence. The king was sitting on a stool, or ottoman, covered with brocade, and inlaid with gold and ivory; while on the floor was spread a gorgeous carpet.

The captain was well satisfied with the interview. He told the king that the Portuguese were from one of the greatest and most enterprising nations in Europe; that King Manuel was powerful, and had mighty armies and fleets; that Vasco da Gama had set sail more than a year before; that they had been endangered ever since by frequent tempests, many hardships, and much treachery; and that Vasco was fully resolved never to return home until India had been reached. The aged king responded kindly, and so impressed Coello with his sincerity and good faith, that when he returned, and recounted what had passed, Vasco's suspicions almost wholly vanished.

It was on a bright, sunny morning that Vasco and Paulo set out in one of their large boats to go near the shore, and there hold an interview with the King of Melinda. The waters of the roadstead glistened in the sun's rays. The town was all alive with gayly-dressed people, who thronged along the quays, and covered the reef with a dense and excited mass. The walls of the town, the caravels, and the ships anchored near, were gay with flags, standards, and streamers, fluttering in the light breeze; and the country round about was clothed in the luxuriant green and ample foliage of the African spring-time. The two boats, as they started away from the ships, were a sight to behold. Vasco and Paulo, attired in cloaks of crimson satin, with plumed caps, and swords, sat upon chairs covered with crimson velvet; while beneath their feet were spread brilliantly-colored carpets. Over the sides of the boats hung woollen rugs, on which sat the men who had been chosen as the retinues of the two captains. Each boat carried two cannon, loaded, and pointed outward; and from each floated the royal standard of Portugal.

They were rapidly rowed to the edge of the quay. There stood the old king, with his long, sweeping white beard, surrounded by his swarthy court, waiting to receive them. Vasco and Paulo rose from their chairs, and saluted him with low bows and uncovered heads. An immense crowd of Moors and Arabs observed them from every point of view, and greeted them with loud acclamations.

They were still too far off, however, to enable the king to converse with them: so he ordered his men to take him to Vasco's boat. Here a chair was placed for him; and Vasco, kneeling, made signs to him to sit. Paulo having gone into his brother's boat, and the African slave who spoke Arabic being in attendance as interpreter, the king and the captains soon engaged in an animated talk.

"Sire," said Paulo da Gama, whom his brother asked to speak, "we are deeply grateful for the honor you do us at this moment. We are anxious to be your friends and servants; and we shall be bounden to you if it pleases you to establish peace and friendship with our liege lord, the King of Portugal."

"God knows," replied the king, "that I have already resolved upon this in my heart. It is what I pray for, and greatly desire; and I affirm, on my allegiance to the Prophet, that I will maintain, as long as I live, a brotherhood with your sovereign."

Vasco, upon this, knelt, and kissed the king's

hand; but he raised him up again. And now the crews shouted out, "Welcome, O king! The Lord be praised!"

The trumpets were sounded, and echoed among the walls; and then the deep booming of the cannon was heard. The people on shore were this time less alarmed than astonished at the noise, and pressed forward to listen to the unwonted reverberation.

Vasco da Gama now approached the king, and offering him a magnificent sword, the scabbard of which was enamelled with gold, a lance of gilded iron, and a buckler of crimson satin sewn with gold-thread, said, —

"It is the custom, sire, for our king to present arms to any new friend or brother whom he adopts: these arms are given that you may defend yourself with them from all enemies. The sword is a token of knighthood, the greatest of earthly honors; and so, whoever breaks a friendship established by the gift of the sword, loses his honor forever. Therefore, sire, we give you this sword and these arms in the name of our king; and we promise to always maintain with you sincere peace and friendship."

"I promise and swear by my faith," replied the king, "to always keep peace and friendship with my new brother of Portugal; and this I now say before all my people."

Vasco then begged the king to persuade the pilot from Mozambique, and the Moor Davane, to be faithful to him, and guide him safely to India; for he wished to go soon, and reach India as soon as possible.

"Oh!" returned the king, laughing, "you must not depart for a while yet, but rest yourselves here. I will advise you what course to take, and to-morrow I will tell you more about it." With this Vasco and Paulo took leave of him, and returned to their ships, where they were met by cheers and the loud tooting of trumpets.

Vasco was now convinced that the King of Melinda was sincere, and did not meditate any treachery or snare against the Portuguese; and he no longer hesitated when the king once more sent him a second invitation to come on shore.

The next day, therefore, he proceeded to the quay, attended by twelve of his men handsomely dressed. He was received by a number of courtiers, who at once conducted him to the royal palace. At the door he was welcomed by the king himself, who embraced him; while Vasco kneeled, and saluted the king with a low bow.

His royal host conducted him within, and invited him to sit beside him on a raised dais covered with silk. Here the conversation of the day before was continued, the interpreter standing respectfully below the dais.

The king told Vasco that he had better not go to Cambay, but to some other port of India.

"The things you seek for are not to be found at Cambay," he said; "or at least they cost much there. But I will give you pilots who will conduct you to the great city of Calicut; for near there grow pepper and ginger, and all other drugs are brought there from every clime. Your broker Davane must go with you; for he knows the price of every thing, and so you will not be cheated."

To all that the king said, Davane, who had come with Vasco, nodded assent. The king then turned to the Moor, and asked him if he would not continue his journey with the Portuguese to Calicut; to which Davane replied, without hesitation, —

"Sire, I should rejoice to go to Calicut, or, for

the matter of that, the world over, with the Portuguese. I have seen much of them, and have been long in their company; and they have treated me excellently well. And I know that the captain is generous, and will abundantly reward me."

"Assuredly I will," returned Vasco, thanking the faithful Moor; "and so well, that, wherever the Portuguese go hereafter in these regions, people will hasten to serve them. And I promise you, sire, that, on my return from India, I will come here again to tell you all that has happened to us, that you may rejoice with us in our good fortune, or share in our grief if our fortune is ill."

Vasco then apprised the king that the ships had fallen short of biscuits, and asked if wheat, with which to make them, was to be had in Melinda. The king not understanding what he meant by "wheat," a boat was sent out to the "San Raphael" to get some.

When he saw it, the king said there was none grown in that country, but that the Cambay merchants brought a little of it to Melinda to be used for the royal table; and that as much as could be found Vasco should have.

"I wish it, sire, as soon as possible," said Vasco, "as I am anxious to depart without delay."

"That you cannot do," returned the king. "You must wait at least three months before crossing the Indian Ocean."

"Why so?" asked Vasco in astonishment.

"Because the winds will not be favorable for your voyage till then. You must sail with the monsoon, or trade-winds. They are now contrary, blowing from the east; and it will be three months before they shift around and set in from the west. At this season there are fearful storms, and you would surely be lost. It is most dangerous to cross the ocean in the face of the contrary trade-winds."

This unwelcome piece of news was a surprise to Vasco, who was extremely chagrined to find that he must lose so much time, and postpone his longed-for arrival in India to so late a period. He had not heard of the trade-winds; and this new obstacle, while it did not discourage him, made him sad and anxious.

Bidding his royal host adieu, he returned to the "San Raphael," and found, when he got there, a new proof of the king's generosity and good will. A boat had been sent out, laden not only with big copper kettles full of boiled rice, but a number of sheep roasted whole, some excellent butter, wheat and rice cakes, some boiled and roasted chickens, vegetables, figs, cocoanuts, and sugar-canes.

There was enough for all the crews, as well as the captains and officers; and while Vasco, Paulo, and Coello sat down to a table groaning with good things, the men gathered on deck, and feasted right merrily. Vasco hastened to send the king, in return, some preserved pears in silver basins, and a fork to eat them with; first eating some of the pears in presence of the king's servant, to show that they were not poisoned. This servant was told to apprise the king that the preserves were to be eaten with water, after dinner.

Vasco informed his brother-captains of what he had learned from the king, and they all deplored the necessity of waiting so long a time at Melinda. They feared that the king's disposition towards them might change, and that false and hostile stories might reach him from Mozambique and Mombaza. In order that this might not happen, they resolved that none of the sailors should go on shore except the sick, who needed change of scene and occupation; and that the Moor Davane should be told to remain always with the king, so that he might contradict any evil reports that should reach their royal friend.

Calling Davane to him, Vasco said, —

"I pray you go to the king, and be always near him; for, while you are there, no Moor will dare to speak evil of us. The Moors of the coast are, no doubt, jealous lest we become their rivals in trade; and will do all they can to poison the king's mind against us. Since we are forced to stay here so long, it is best to foster the friendship which the king now shows us."

With this the Moor, smiling, said to Vasco, —

"Captain, how is it, that, I being a Moor, you repose so much trust in me?"

"My heart tells me that you are a true friend," returned Vasco. "You have done us many good turns, and never a bad one; and so I am led to confide in you."

One of the Caffres who was standing by, and understood what was said, grinned, and said to Vasco, —

"Sir, this man very *taibo;*" taibo meaning "very good."

This pleased Davane very much, and he patted the Caffre good-naturedly on the back. From that time the sailors got into the habit of calling Davane "Taibo."

Vasco was very grateful to the good Moor for his fidelity, and now showed his gratitude by throwing a heavy gold chain around his neck, which Davane, delighted, hastened off to show the king. The king, equally impressed with Davane's goodness, followed Vasco's example, and made him a present of a silken pelisse. Obeying the orders of Vasco, the Moor took up his abode in the royal palace. The king grew very familiar with him, and, being a very jolly old fellow, sat and joked with him by the hour together.

Meanwhile Vasco made the best of the situation, and prepared to remain at Melinda until the trade-winds became favorable. There was, indeed, much that might be done during the three months before them, and no lack of work and recreation with which to make the weeks pass rapidly.

Calling together the masters and pilots, Vasco told them of the delay, and gave orders as to how the time should be employed.

The ships were in some need of repair, and it was necessary to get in provisions for a voyage, which, should the weather prove unfavorable, might be long and tedious.

Once more the ships were heeled over, and the sides thoroughly calked. The decks and upper parts were made water-tight with pitch; and ropes were twisted of a thread made by the natives from the outer husks of cocoanuts, which proved to be excellent for the purpose, as they could be stretched like India-rubber, and were yet stronger in salt water than the cables brought by the Portuguese.

Vasco's wisdom in making his sailors learn to be artisans before they left Lisbon was now amply confirmed. Some of them set to work making hawsers and rigging; others proved to be skilful calkers; yet others employed themselves on such carpentry-work as the ships needed inside and out. Much of the work of making ropes and rigging was done on shore; and this brought a crowd of curious Moors around the sailors every day.

At the same time, the work of provisioning the ships went actively on. They were supplied with an abundance of fresh water, which was obtained without difficulty from the streams near Melinda.

Meat, vegetables, meal, and fruit were brought on board, and stowed away for future use; and the ship-boy of the "San Raphael," accompanied by a negro interpreter, went on shore every day to make purchases.

In this provisioning of the ships, the Portuguese were greatly befriended by the king, who ordered a crier to go through the city to proclaim that nothing should be sold to the strangers for more than it was worth; and that, if any merchant overcharged them, the king would cause his house to be burned to the ground.

Vasco and his brother-captains now went fearlessly on shore as often as they pleased; and the king, remaining steadfast in his friendship, would have them dine with him, take them on excursions around the city and in the suburbs, and promenade with them in a large pleasure-garden at a little distance from his palace.

One day, after the Portuguese had been at Melinda some weeks, the king told Vasco that he was very curious to see the ships, and go all over them. They had now been repaired and put in good trim; and Vasco hastened to take the king's hint, and invite him on board. A day for the visit was fixed, and Vasco ordered that every preparation should be made to give his royal guest a fitting reception.

CHAPTER XII.

DEPARTURE FROM MELINDA.

THE ships looked very gay and imposing on the morning appointed for the King of Melinda's visit. The decks glistened, so thoroughly had they been washed by the sailors. Perfumes were scattered about them; green boughs were disposed in one place and another to give a holiday look; flags floated from the masts and rigging; on the quarter-decks figured stuffs from Flanders, carpets, and brilliantly-colored rugs, were spread; while here and there were placed stands of lances, with newly-burnished and glittering points; and swords, cross-bows, breast-plates, and daggers were hung in graceful arrangement at the masts and sides.

Meanwhile the good old king was resolved to do honor to his new friends by going to them in all the state and magnificence he could command. Arrayed in a long coat of crimson damask lined with green satin, and wearing a splendid turban sewn with jewels, he waited on the quay, surrounded by a gorgeous group of nobles, for Vasco's boats to come off and take him to the ships.

Vasco and Paulo, when every thing was ready, proceeded to the shore in their boats. In that of Paulo was placed a chair covered with crimson velvet fringed with gold-lace. On the bottom of the boat was spread a rich carpet, and a handsome banner of white and red damask floated from the bow. When they reached the shore, the king took his place on the chair, expressing his regret that the captains were obliged to stand.

Vasco replied, that, in his country, it was not the custom for any one to sit in the presence of the monarch.

A large fleet of boats, some Moorish canoes, some belonging to the merchant-ships in the harbor, accompanied the king and captains to the Portuguese ships; and the air was filled with the strange music of the instruments that were carried in them, and the loud noise of the Portuguese trumpets.

When the gay little fleet of boats reached the "San Raphael," the cannon boomed forth a deafening welcome. But the king was not yet ready to go on board. He asked Vasco to order the sailors to row around the ships, so that he might see the outsides; and, as they did so, the king plied Vasco with many questions as to the rigging and construction.

Then he ascended on board the "San Raphael," where the crew, dressed in their best attire, stood in rows, and with uncovered heads, to receive him.

The king and his retinue being invited to sit on the quarter-deck, Vasco pointed out to him the various parts of the rigging, and explained their uses. Then he conducted his royal guest about the ship, showing him the hold, cabins, and store-rooms. In Vasco's own cabin a dainty luncheon was spread, with meats, preserves, olives, and wine, of which the king partook heartily, and without the slightest hesitation. He expressed his surprise and delight at all that he saw, and exclaimed, "If these men use silver, their king must not use any thing but gold."

The meal over, Vasco brought a gilt hand-basin

and ewer, and offered to pour water on the king's hands to wash them. But this the king would not permit. He called one of his own attendants, who poured out the water, with which he washed his hands and mouth, drying them with a napkin embroidered with gold.

Vasco then made a present of the ewer and basin to the king, who at first declined them; but Vasco told him, that, as he had used them, no one else could, according to etiquette: whereat the king expressed his delight, exclaiming that no king in India had such splendid vessels.

The old monarch next went on board the "San Gabriel," and, having inspected it, returned to the shore, declaring that he never spent a more pleasant day. Vasco took care to send after him a present of cloths and caps for the king and his ministers, which completed their satisfaction.

"Nothing," cried the king to his courtiers, "is wanting to these men to achieve whatever they desire."

With the leisurely preparations for departure, the frequent festivities with the old king and his court, the excursions on shore, and visits to the Christian merchant-men, the time passed rapidly away; and, before Vasco knew it, months had gone, and July had come.

The king kept his promise to supply him with two pilots who were familiar with the passage to India, — one for each of the ships. One of these pilots, named Canaca, belonged to an Indian ship, and, on going on board, was found not only to be already acquainted with the astrolabes and quadrants used by Europeans in navigation, but also to have other nautical instruments which the Portuguese had never before seen. He brought with him a map of the coast of India, with the bearings carefully marked upon it; and seemed, indeed, to be quite as well versed in navigation as the Portuguese themselves. The king also succeeded in persuading the Mozambique pilot, who had been so indignant at being put and kept in irons, to swallow the affront, and do his best to serve Vasco da Gama faithfully, which he agreed to do.

Several days before the departure of the ships, the king invited the captains to a great banquet in his palace, at the same time despatching a number of boats with food for the crews. He further showed his good will by sending some native carpenters to construct tanks in the ships for holding the fresh water. These tanks were not nailed, but fastened tight with cocoanut-thread; and the cracks were plastered with pitch. Four of them were put into each ship, and each tank held thirty pipes of water. The Portuguese were, therefore, in no danger of getting out of water again until they should safely reach the Indian coast.

The captains went on shore every day to visit the king; and, when they were about to depart, Vasco said to him, —

"Since, sire, both sea and land have their perils, we wish to leave here a mark which will remain in your city to call our sojourn with you to mind. This mark is a column, with the name of our king upon it; for, in every country that is friendly to him, we place these columns as tokens of his good faith."

"Put up the column as soon as you please," returned the king. "You shall set it at the gate of my palace."

"But if it stands within the city," said Vasco, "it will not be seen by the ships that arrive in port. I pray you, let it be set up where it will be plainly visible from the sea."

"Very well: choose whatever spot you like best, and set it up there. But why did you not erect this column when you first came?"

"Our sovereign," replied Vasco, "commanded us only to set it up in a country which we were sure was friendly and sincere; and we could not know your disposition, sire, when we arrived. But now your goodness has made it sure."

A white marble shaft was forthwith brought from the "San Raphael," with a handsome pedestal and carved top, on the lower part of which were engraved and gilded the words "King Manuel." Vasco, looking about for a place where to erect it, espied a round hill which rose above the port, on the southern side of the city, and there resolved to set up the column.

It was put in position by the Portuguese, assisted by some Moorish stone-masons. When this was done, a tent was erected just by the column, and beneath the tent was placed an altar. The altar was covered with a rich cloth, and upon it rested a statue of the Virgin Mary.

Three priests said mass beneath the tent, the captains and crews standing or kneeling around, and crowds of the people of Melinda gathering to witness the solemn ceremony. The column was dedicated to the friendship between King Manuel and the King of Melinda; and, when the service was over, the Portuguese returned to their ships.

Vasco da Gama gave some money to the Melinda pilots to be left with their families, and took occasion to present the king with about seven hundred dollars in gold Portuguese coins, done up in a handkerchief. The ship-boy who had been so useful in making the purchases for the ships, and who was one of the convicts Vasco had brought with him, was then consigned to the king, to remain at Melinda until the ships returned from India.

"Your life will be quite safe here," said Vasco to the ship-boy; "for the King of Melinda is a true friend of ours. Be sure and keep your eyes open: look about you well, and see and learn every thing you can about this country and its people, against my return. If you choose, you may travel about among the other countries of the coast; and don't fail to treasure up all the knowledge you acquire. If you do this, I will take you safely back to Portugal, where you shall be one of the gentlemen of the royal household, as a reward for your fidelity."

The ship-boy thanked Vasco, and readily consented to stay at Melinda.

The time had now come for bidding the good old king and his fair city farewell. It was the 5th of August; and the 6th was the day appointed for the Portuguese to sail.

In the afternoon a number of boats came out to the ships, fairly loaded with good things. There were great boxes of biscuit, rice, and butter; there was a quantity of salted mutton; and there were live sheep, fowls, and vegetables, cocoanuts, fruit, and sacks full of sugar. Such was the generous parting gift of the king.

Early the next morning he came out to the ships to bid them all good-by. The old man was really overcome by the prospect of their departure, and embraced Vasco and Paulo affectionately, begging them not to forget to come that way on their return from India. As the royal boat slowly wended its way back to the shore, the trumpets sounded, the cannon roared, and the crews cheered, and shouted "Lord God be with you, farewell!" while Vasco and Paulo stood on the quarter-decks, and waved their hands to the king, the people on the crowded quays and reef, and the crews of the ships which lay at anchor all around them.

The priests now appeared in their robes; and, as all hands knelt on the decks, a solemn prayer went up to heaven for a safe voyage and a happy return.

Vasco, in a loud voice, gave the order to loosen the sails; and, with a fair wind blowing in the right direction (for the trade-winds had now shifted, and were favorable), the "San Raphael" and the "San Gabriel" sped gayly out of the roadstead of Melinda.

They were about to stretch off into the vast and unknown ocean which lay between them and the crowning object of their perilous voyage. Until then, they had only been skirting the African coast, seldom losing sight of land, and constantly occupied by new sights and stirring adventures: now they were to brave the dangers of strange seas, filling the wide space of nearly two thousands miles between the African and the Asiatic shore.

Happily, in Vasco da Gama the ships had a

commander with a cool, clear head, and a strong, confident, and heroic heart; and one and all looked forward with lively hope and cheerful expectation to the voyage before them.

CHAPTER XIII.

INDIA AT LAST.

WITH what eager, hopeful heart Vasco da Gama looked forward to this voyage across the Indian Ocean! How long seemed the days in traversing it! and how vast seemed these uncertain seas! If he could only at last reach the welcome shores of India, the haven he had now been seeking, amid every danger, for nearly a year and a half; if he could make a treaty of friendship with the sovereign of that country, and load his caravels with its riches, —with what a thrill of pride and joy would he turn his prows again towards home!

How exultantly would he enter the harbor of Lisbon with his precious cargoes and his glorious news! He would then be hailed, not only by his countrymen, but by all Europe, as the discoverer of the mysterious passage which had been sought so long; he would be named as the equal and rival of Columbus; no honors would be too great for his deserts; and his exploits would go down in history, making his name forever famous, and his deeds the admiration of remote generations.

We may well believe that these glowing thoughts filled the ambitious soul of Vasco da Gama as the friendly trade-winds sped the "San Raphael" and the "San Gabriel" over the unknown ocean. Often, sitting upon his quarter-deck, he gazed over the waves, as if yearning to behold the promised land of India. Eagerly he listened to the words of the Melinda pilots, as they assured him that they were on the right track, and that it would not be many days ere the peaks of the Malabar mountains would gladden their sight. The two caravels were able, thanks to the favorable weather, to keep close together; and sometimes they were so near each other, that Vasco could talk with his gentle brother Paulo from deck to deck.

Both the pilots and the sailors were in the best of spirits; and no thought of turning back, or of resisting the captain's will, seemed to enter their heads. Vasco spent much of his time talking with the Moors on board through interpreters, and learned as much as he could from them about the country and the people of India. Some of them had been there, and could tell him much that was interesting and valuable for him to know.

The voyage was, almost without interruption, a pleasant one. The trade-winds blew the caravels steadily in the right direction; and, if a gale swept over the waters, it only served to carry them more rapidly on their way. Thanks to the thorough repairs which both ships had undergone, no accident or mishap overtook either of them. The days were, for the most part, sunny and temperate; and the nights pleasantly cool, freshened by light west breezes.

Thus they went on day after day, no incident occurring to delay their steady progress, and nothing happening to vary the monotony of the voyage. When they had been out from Melinda about a week, a pilot one evening pointed to the heavens, and exclaimed that he saw the north star; and, looking southward, they found that they could see the glittering white constellations grouped about the south pole.

The discovery that the north star was visible rejoiced the pilots; for they could now direct the course of the caravels more accurately, and be sure that they were not losing time by varying from the direct and shortest track.

One morning, when the voyage had lasted about nineteen days, Canaca, the Melinda pilot, came to Vasco da Gama with an air of satisfaction on his grave, dark face, and, pulling off his cap, said, —

"Captain, I am sure we are very near the coast of India. It would not surprise me if we should see land to-morrow morning."

Vasco's heart bounded in his breast at these words, and he uttered a profound thanksgiving to God. He thanked the pilot also, and promised that he should not regret it if it should turn out that he was a true prophet. Very likely the gallant captain did not sleep soundly that night. Early in the morning he was on deck with his men; and the eyes of all were straining towards the east, each eager to catch the first glimpse of land.

A number of sailors were perched on the main-tops as lookouts. Vasco was at his usual post on the quarter-deck. Suddenly a loud cry was heard from several mouths, —

"Land, land, land!"

A moment after, the pilot Canaca came running up, and, prostrating himself at Vasco's feet, pointed with trembling finger towards the horizon in the east.

"Behold, captain! — the land of India!"

A confused shout of joy on both decks; wild cries of delight; a frantic rushing to and fro of sailors, some with tears running down their cheeks; a moment in which there seemed to be no officers, no order on board, but in which Vasco, Paulo, Coello, the sailors, the Moors, the convicts, seemed to be simply a crowd of weary wanderers who now saw the goal of all their hopes, — and then the voice of the captain rose above the noise, and there was silence.

"There," he said, pointing eastward, — "there is India! Let us first thank the bounteous Heaven that has guided us hither."

So saying, Vasco da Gama fell upon his knees, and all the rest followed his example. No word of prayer was spoken; the hearts bowed before God were too full for utterance: but it is certain

"Behold, Captain! the Land of India!" Page 166.

that in every one Vasco's silent prayer was heartily echoed.

When the solemn thanksgiving was over, and they once more gazed eastward, the great news was confirmed: there could be no doubt about it. What had been but a filmy streak, a faint, hazy line in the horizon, had now grown into the substance of blue though indistinct mountain eminences, rising apparently from the pale waters, and softly reflecting the rays of the bright sun. Canaca thought the shore twenty four or five miles distant; and, on making soundings, found the water forty-five fathoms deep.

Just then there came up a blinding rain, which, for a while, shut out the blessed view of the land; but when, in the course of an hour or two, the shower had spent its force, they found that they had meanwhile rapidly approached the coast.

Vasco da Gama, grateful to the Moorish pilots for their fidelity, called them to him, and gave each a robe of red cloth and a goodly sum of money, which they received with many low bows and with evident delight.

It was afternoon when the ships approached near enough to see objects on the shore, and the broad shining beaches stretching away in the distance. They ran along the coast, and ere long came in sight of a good-sized town, nestled in a bay, with thatched houses, and a number of fishing-boats, some of which were at anchor, and others moving about. The inhabitants of this town seemed greatly astonished to see the ships, and the fishing-boats came quite near to examine them.

At first, Vasco da Gama mistook this town for Calicut, and was greatly disappointed to see so rude a looking place; for he had heard a great deal of the splendor of Calicut, its noble buildings and temples, and its riches.

The pilot Canaca soon undeceived him.

"That place," said he, "is called Cananor. I know the country well. But be not discouraged, captain: Calicut, the great city, is only twelve leagues distant, to the southward."

From what Vasco da Gama learned afterward, it appeared that the people of Cananor had other reasons besides curiosity for regarding his ships, as they sailed along the coast, with amazement and terror.

Many years before, there had lived at Cananor

a great magician, famous for his marvellous predictions. This magician had foretold to the King of Cananor, that, at some future time, the whole of India would be conquered and ruled over by a king who lived a great way off, whose subjects were white, and were a fierce people, though friendly to those who treated them well.

When, therefore, the king and his people saw the Portuguese ships, and the white men in them, they feared that they were the men meant by the ancient seer. So the king called his astrologers, and asked if this were true. Consulting their oracles, they replied that these were indeed the people who would conquer India.

The king, believing all that they said, and bearing in mind the prophecy that the white men would deal gently with those who proved themselves friendly, resolved to make peace with the Portuguese as soon as he had the opportunity; and sent messengers on to Calicut to learn all they could about the strangers, and to report what they heard to him.

Meanwhile the ships ran along the coast southward; and that night Vasco da Gama went to bed, well assured that the next day he should at last gaze on the famed city of Calicut.

So, indeed, it happened. The morning was fine, and the wind favorable; and before noon the city loomed before their eyes. Its domes and minarets glittered in the sunlight; its broad quays seemed full of life; and in the bay upon which Calicut was situated floated many ships from all parts of the East.

Vasco da Gama was, however, too wise to venture within the bay, or to cast anchor in too near a proximity to the shore. He was by no means sure of the reception he would meet with, nor would he venture to brave a possible hostility with his two frail little ships and his handful of men.

At the entrance of the bay was a small town, called Capocate, or Capucad, about six miles from Calicut. Here there was safe anchorage at a convenient distance from the city, and yet near enough to enable the boats to go easily back and forth.

It was now sundown; and Vasco da Gama thought it best to wait till morning before attempting to enter into any communication with those on shore.

Meanwhile he called together his brother Paulo, Coello, and the faithful Moor Davane, and consulted with them how to deal with the King of Calicut.

At first, Vasco proposed to go himself on shore the next morning, to present himself before the potentate, and frankly to tell him the purpose for which he had come to India.

But Davane warned him by no means to do this, as the king might be hostile; and, if he were, no one could tell what he would do. The best way, Davane said, was to first demand hostages for his safety, as this was the custom of the East.

Then Vasco and the other captains resolved that they would employ a fiction to awe the king, and to deter him from putting into execution any hostile design he might conceive. They would tell him that the King of Portugal had sent out a great fleet of fifty vessels; that the two ships, "San Gabriel" and "San Raphael," had separated from the rest of the fleet in a storm; and that they had come to Calicut to await the arrival of the other ships.

The king would then be afraid to deal perfidiously with them, lest the fleet should come, and, finding what had happened, should bombard and destroy the city.

The next morning, no sooner was the eun fairly up than a number of boats surrounded the two ships. In them were natives, with dusky skins, and naked, except that they wore cloths of various colors about their loins. They seemed very curious to know who the Portuguese were, and whence they came. The shore, too, was soon crowded with a multitude of people, who gazed at the two ships as if they were some unknown monsters of the deep that had suddenly appeared to them.

Among the boats were some fishing-smacks, and these came up close to the ships ; and Vasco ordered his men to call to the fishermen, and offer to buy their fish.

The native fishermen went on board at once, and were delighted to receive some silver coins (which they took care to test by biting them with their teeth) in exchange for their wares. The Moorish pilots told them the story which Vasco da Gama had concocted about the fleet of fifty ships, which they went off and repeated to the people on shore.

Their story speedily came to the ears of the King of Calicut, who was called the Zamorin; and he told the fishermen to return to the ships, carrying figs, cocoanuts, and chickens, and to find out all they could.

Presently a boat laden with wood to sell came up to the "San Raphael;" but, as there was plenty of wood on board, Vasco declined to buy it. The men in the boat were going away much disappointed, when Vasco had them called back, and ordered some money to be distributed among them.

Davane asked him why he did this.

"Because," replied Vasco, "they are poor men, and came to sell their wood, and were going off disappointed. So I have given them money, that their labor may not be lost. It is thus I am wont to treat those who try to serve me."

The natives were told this reply of the captain, and, going ashore, repeated it to their people, which favorably impressed them with the Portuguese.

For three days, nothing was done except to engage in trade with the fishermen. On the fourth day, however, a large boat came out to the "San Raphael," bringing a man of high birth, whom they called a Nair, — a messenger from the Zamorin.

This Nair was naked, except that he wore a white cloth about his loins. He carried a small round shield, some wooden slings, and a short naked sword with an iron hilt. His hair was matted close to his head. He was tall, well-proportioned, and very dark.

He refused to go on board, but spoke to Vasco da Gama through an interpreter from his boat. His message from the Zamorin was to ask who the strangers were, and what they wanted in Calicut.

Vasco replied that he had not sent a message to the Zamorin, since he had not until now had his consent to do so. But he would send a messenger on shore with the Nair, who would answer the Zamorin.

The Moor Davane accordingly went back with the Nair, and, on being ushered into the king's presence, told him the story which Vasco da Gama had instructed him to tell. He said that the Portuguese had come from the greatest Christian king in the world, who had sent a fleet of fifty ships, from which these two had separated; that they had come to make peace and friendship with the Zamorin, and to buy cargoes of pepper and drugs with the rich cloths, gold, and silver which they had brought with them.

The Zamorin seemed much astonished to hear this, and began to talk earnestly with his courtiers. Meanwhile one of his officers asked the Moor how he came to be with the Portuguese.

Davane told him, and added an account of the noble and generous presents which Vasco had given to the King of Melinda. The Zamorin, it appeared, was very covetous, and, when he heard this, eagerly assured Davane that Vasco was welcome at Calicut.

"Tell him," added the potentate, "that I will fill his ships with as much pepper and as many drugs as he can carry away with him."

He then sent Davane back to the "San Raphael," taking good care to provide him with a present of figs and chickens for the captain.

The return of the Moor with his friendly messages greatly pleased the brothers, who rejoiced in the prospect of securing the Zamorin's good will, and of obtaining a valuable cargo with which to return to Portugal.

They regaled themselves upon the provisions which the Zamorin had sent, and resolved to send

Davane to him with other messages the next day. Davane, accordingly, returned in the morning to the city, and told the Zamorin that the captain was unwilling to enter upon trading until he had made a secure treaty of peace; and begged the Zamorin to send hostages, so that the captain might go on shore and visit him in person, and deliver the letter he had from the King of Portugal.

Meanwhile the Zamorin, who had seemed so eager to welcome Vasco, had not only consulted with his advisers, but had become subject to a powerful influence which was brought to bear in hostility to the Portuguese. While Vasco da Gama slept in the serene confidence that his troubles were at an end, and that he had already secured peace and friendship with the Zamorin, powerful enemies were working upon the mind of the sovereign, and doing every thing in their power to persuade him to send the Portuguese away.

In order to understand who these enemies were, and what the cause of their hostility was, we must give a brief account of this city of Calicut, the people who lived in it, and the manners and customs which existed there.

CHAPTER XIV.

SOMETHING ABOUT CALICUT.

CALICUT, at the time of Vasco da Gama's voyage, was one of the largest, richest, and most famous cities of India. Its renown had reached Europe, and it was known that there dwelt one of the most powerful potentates in the East. Situated on the south-western coast of India, with a good harbor, it was the centre of a very active and prosperous trade. Hither came the great Arabian and Egyptian merchants to seek for the precious spices, drugs, and other merchandise which India afforded; and hither, too, came the Hindoos from the interior for the goods brought by those merchants, and sent even from distant Venice and Genoa.

Calicut was and is situated in a low, flat country, with occasional high hills rising from the level, and overlooking the ocean. It is said that the whole district around was once covered with water; and there was a legend that the god of the ocean caused the waters to recede, and leave a large space, for the benefit of the Brahmin priests, who prayed for this favor.

Some centuries before Vasco's arrival, the Moors of Mecca in Arabia, coasting about in their rude vessels, had discovered India, and had come as far as Calicut. They were an enterprising race, and, finding the trade with India profitable, continued to visit the coast with many vessels for a long period of years, carrying cargoes to and fro. Gradually these Arabs began to settle at Calicut and other towns along the coasts; and while they traded with the natives, who were a race very inferior to them in energy and intelligence, they took advantage of their opportunity to make converts to the Mohammedan religion.

There reigned at that time in Malabar, the province of which Calicut was the chief city, a prince named Permaloo, who, having been appointed governor of it by the Rajah of Chaldesh (the sovereign of that part of India), had defied the Rajah's authority, and set up in Malabar an independent kingdom of his own.

Prince Permaloo was worked upon by the Arabs, until they converted him to the Mohammedan faith. This caused his nobles to revolt; and Permaloo, tired of the cares of sovereignty, divided up his dominions among various kinsmen and chieftains. The city and neighborhood of Calicut he awarded to a low-born favorite, a cowherd, who had behaved very valiantly in the wars against the Rajah, and who, assuming the government, was awarded the title of Zamorin. Permaloo retired for the rest of his days to Mecca.

From the cowherd were descended the succeeding Zamorins, or rulers of Calicut. These princes, in spite of the fate of Permaloo, who had been forced to abdicate because of his conversion to the Mohammedan faith, encouraged the Arabs to trade and to settle in Calicut, and offered no obstacle to their converting as many natives as they pleased. They were glad to have the Arabs bring their riches to the city, and endow it with a prosperous trade; and the Arabs took care to keep the good will of the Zamorins by making them frequent and costly presents.

The trade between the Arabs and the Hindoos

included a great variety of precious and useful articles. In the warehouses of Calicut were to be found not only spices and drugs, but precious stones, musk, lacquer and earthen ware, gold, amber, wax and ivory, cotton and silk cloths, and cloths-of-gold, grain, carpets, copper, quicksilver, vermilion, alum, coral, rose-water, preserves, and provisions in bewildering profusion.

The city was large enough to occupy a space several miles square. Its trade was so prosperous, that many of the Arab and Moorish merchants who resided there owned as many as fifty ships; and it was not rare for five or six hundred ships to visit its harbor in the course of a winter.

The princes, or Zamorins, in the course of years waxed rich and strong. They became able to raise armies of one hundred thousand men, and succeeded in subduing and making vassals of the two neighboring Kings of Coulan and Cananor.

They belonged to the priestly rank of Brahmins; and it was an ancient law of Calicut, that the Zamorins must die in the pagoda, or temple of the Hindoo gods. These potentates were accustomed to array themselves in silk or cotton gowns below the middle, being naked above. Sometimes, however, they wore scarlet or cloth-of-gold tunics above the waist. They shaved their beards, and wore only a mustache, but, unlike the Moors, left their heads unshaven.

The Zamorins never married, but had a concubine, whom they could put away at pleasure, and take another. Their children did not succeed them, but brother succeeded brother; and, there being none of these, the sons of the Zamorin's sisters succeeded him.

Many were the curious customs which prevailed at Calicut, a few of which may be described. The Zamorins were very courageous and warlike, and often led their troops into battle, exposing themselves in the front ranks. If a Zamorin was killed, on the third day after death his body was taken into a field, and placed on a pyre of sandal and other precious woods, his relatives and nobles all standing by. The body was burned amid the lamentations of the multitude, and the ashes were gathered and buried. Then all the relatives, even the children, set to shaving every part of their bodies; this being a token of great mourning. In the ensuing fortnight they were forbidden to chew betel, a favorite practice in that region;

and, if any of them broke this rule, his lips were cut with a sharp knife.

At the end of the fortnight the new Zamorin was sworn into office in presence of the court. As he took the oath, he held a burning candle, on which was a gold ring, with his right hand, touching the ring with the fingers of his left. Then grains of rice were thrown upon him, prayers were chanted by the priests, and the assemblage prostrated themselves three times before the sun.

This ended, all were permitted to chew betel, except the new monarch, who was enjoined to mourn for his predecessor through an entire year, during which period he could neither chew betel, eat fish or meat, shave his beard, or even cut his nails. He was obliged to content himself with eating but once a day, taking a bath first; and certain hours of each day he set apart for prayer. The year of mourning over, the Zamorin celebrated a sort of mass for the repose of the soul of his predecessor before an immense concourse of the people, and then his privations were ended.

It has already been related that a man of high birth and military bearing, called a Nair, visited Vasco da Gama in the harbor as the messenger of the Zamorin. The Nairs constituted a distinct rank and caste at Calicut. They comprised the upper class of the natives. They went naked and with bare feet, wearing only a painted cloth from the waist to the knees, and a small turban on their heads. For arms they bore bows and arrows, spears, daggers, and rude short-swords; and they were a valiant and well-disciplined body of men.

The Nairs were supported entirely at the Zamorin's charge, each having a page attached to his person; and they engaged in no occupation except that of a soldier. They were not allowed to marry, but, like the Zamorin, had concubines; and their property and titles passed in the same line of succession as that already described of the Zamorins. The Zamorin could not make a Nair of a peasant, the Nairs being such by descent. A Nair could not be thrown into prison for any offence, and was only subject to the death-penalty if he killed another Nair or a cow (which was a sacred animal among them), or spoke evil of the Zamorin. When one of them committed the latter offence, the Zamorin would send several other Nairs, who would kill the offender wherever they met him, and attach to his body the royal order for the execution.

The Nairs were not allowed to bear arms or take part in the wars, until they had been made knights. At seven years old a little Nair began to learn the art of war: his joints were pulled and twisted to make them supple, and then he was taught the use of the various weapons. There were a number of military teachers, called "Panycaes," who were held in high honor, and to whom their scholars were obliged to pay especial respect all the rest of their lives. The Nairs never ceased taking military lessons. Two months in every year they devoted to military practice under the eyes of their masters.

When a Nair was ready to become a knight — that is, to enter upon active military service — he resorted to the Zamorin, attended by all his relations, and made him a present of sixty golden coins called "fannons," each fannon being worth about four dollars. Then the Zamorin asked him if he wished to serve, and would do so faithfully; to which he replied, "Yes." The Zamorin thereupon ordered an officer to gird him with a sword, and, putting his right hand upon his head, uttered a short prayer, and then embraced the new knight.

The Nairs looked with contempt on the lower class of the natives, many of whom had been converted to Mohammedanism. These poor people were obliged, in going along the streets or roads, to keep shouting in a loud voice, "Hoo, hoo!" so that, if a Nair were coming along, he might order them to make way for him. If a Nair shouted to them, they hurried into the bushes; for, if they did not make way, the Nair had a right to kill them on the spot.

But the Arabs, who, as we have seen, had grown very rich and powerful in the course of years at Calicut, used their influence with the Zamorin to exempt from ill treatment those of the common people who had turned Mohammedans; and this the Zamorin granted. The result was, that many of these poor peasants, who lived in the bush and in the fields, and ate herbs and land-crabs, embraced the religion of the Arabs, and in this way put themselves out of the power of the tyrannical Nairs.

Calicut was composed mostly of straw huts; but there were many temples, pagodas, palaces, and Arab residences, here and there, which were built of stone and lime, with tiled roofs, and were several stories high. In the suburbs of the city were many delightful orchards and gardens, with palm-groves and fruit-trees, and wells of delicious water. The ships which were seen in its harbor were like those seen by Vasco da Gama on the African coast, — built without nails, the planks and beams being fastened together with cords of the cocoanut husk. The bottoms were flat, as there were no keels to the ships.

The rich and powerful Arab merchants in Calicut had no sooner heard of the arrival of the Portuguese ships outside the harbor than they grew very much alarmed. They feared lest these Europeans should become their rivals in trade, if, indeed, they did not rob them of their trade altogether. They had now no rivals, and were waxing richer and richer by the commerce they carried on. They looked upon the Portuguese ships as the forerunners of fleets which would come from Europe and bear away the rich cargoes which they themselves were in the habit of obtaining.

So the Arabs in Calicut got together, and resolved to do what they could to poison the Zamorin's mind against the Portuguese, and to induce him, through fear, to send the ships away. They despatched messengers to the towns along the coast, and warned their brother Arabs of the danger which threatened their trade; and many Arabs hurried from these towns to Calicut to help their countrymen there to get rid of the Portuguese.

Among the Zamorin's officers was a treasurer, and a minister of justice, who was called the "Gozil." These two men had no little influence over the sovereign; and, being greedy and corrupt, they were both open to bribery.

The principal Arabs resorted, then, to the treasurer and the Gozil, and, making them promises of large sums of money, begged them to arouse the Zamorin's fears and suspicions against the strangers. They engaged them to tell him that the Portuguese, who were rich, had not come thither for the peaceful purposes of trade, but to make conquests of the rich Indian kingdoms; that these ships had been sent out as spies to see whether this could be done; and that doubtless, unless they were ordered away, they would be followed by large fleets, which would come and attack the power of the Zamorin and other Indian potentates.

The two officers listened to the Arabs, and pretended to be convinced by them. They thankfully accepted the presents which the Arabs offered, and promised to tell the king what they said. But, when the officers were alone, they said to each other that they would be cautious, and not say all that had been said to them. They would say just enough to arouse in the Zamorin's mind distrust of the Portuguese, but would leave the way open to take another tack, if, after all, the Zamorin should find it profitable to make friends with the Portuguese, and treat them well. Meanwhile they would get as many presents out of the Arabs as they could.

The Gozil went to the Zamorin, and said enough to make him somewhat wary and suspicious; but the monarch was so covetous of wealth, and was so impressed by what the Moor Davane had told him of the generous deeds of the Portuguese at Melinda, that he resolved to continue his dealings with Vasco da Gama.

The Zamorin was under the influence of what had been said to him by the Gozil, when the Moor Davane came to him the second time, as has been related. He therefore delayed his reply to the request for hostages, but bade Davane return to the ship, and tell the captain to send any one on shore whom he chose; to look about the city, and make purchases; and that whomsoever he sent should be allowed to go and come in safety.

Vasco da Gama was much chagrined to perceive that the Zamorin was suspicious; for he had hoped that there would be no difficulty in making peace with him, and winning his confidence. However, he resolved to make the best of circumstances, and in all things to conduct himself in such a way as to banish distrust from the Indian potentate's mind. It was very important that he should, if possible, conciliate the Zamorin, and succeed in procuring a cargo, so as to show King Manuel, on his return, that his voyage had been triumphant.

On board the "San Raphael" was a convict of unusual intelligence, who had been sentenced for some crime to banishment, but had been allowed to go with Vasco da Gama on his voyage. This man's name was Joan Nunez; and fortunately he understood both Arabic and Hebrew.

Vasco chose Joan Nunez to accompany Davane on shore, telling him to observe every thing narrowly; to listen to all that the people said, but to be very cautious about answering any questions they might ask him. He also warned Joan on no account to separate from Davane, but to keep always close to him ; and he gave him money, and a list of provisions that he wished him to purchase, instructing him to buy no other goods, but only to note what there was in the shops. The next morning, therefore, Joan Nunez and Davane went on shore in one of the boats, and prepared to obey Vasco da Gama's commands.

CHAPTER XV.

ADVENTURES AT CALICUT.

NO sooner had Davane and Joan Nunez stepped upon the quay than they were surrounded by so eager a crowd, anxious to see Joan Nunez (for rarely had these natives seen a white man), that they were almost smothered, and could scarcely push their way through the mass of natives. Joan had to keep a tight hold on Davane's cloak, so as not to be separated from him. Davane, hurrying along, made his way as best he could to the Gozil's house. This great man received them warmly, and gave them free permission to ramble through the city; and, having heard how rudely they had been jostled by the people, he sent one of his servants with them to keep a clear passage.

As they passed along the streets, some of the

Arab merchants saw them. These hastened to persuade the Gozil to detain Joan and Davane in the city over night, so that they might be questioned, and something might be learned from them which the Arabs could use against the Portuguese. This the Gozil, remembering the presents of the Arabs, promised to do.

Joan and Davane were walking leisurely through a long street, gazing at the low shops and bazaars, with their curious wares of ivory and fruit, when suddenly a man came up to them, and, looking hard at Joan, to his great amazement addressed him in Spanish.

"Devil take you!" said the man abruptly. "What brought you here?"

This salutation did not seem very polite; but, in reality, it was the customary form of welcome. The man immediately showed that he did not mean an insult by continuing, —

"Brother, God preserve you!"

Joan, who knew Spanish well, was so much surprised and rejoiced to hear its familiar tones, that at first he did not reply. Then, recovering himself, he said, —

"God give you health, sir!"

The man asked him where he was going.

"We are going," replied Joan, "to sleep at the Gozil's house."

"I pray you do not," responded the man who spoke Spanish, "but come along with me to my house. It will give me joy to have you go there and sleep, and eat as much as you choose."

But the Gozil's servant would not permit them to go until his master's consent had been obtained. The Gozil, when appealed to, readily granted their request; and, when they reached the man's house, he made them merry with a bounteous supper.

He asked Joan where the ships were from, and all about their adventures; and then told him that he himself was a native of Seville, in Spain. He went on to say, that, when a small boy, he had been taken prisoner, and brought to Asia, by some Moors; and that, on regaining his liberty, he had wandered about a great deal, at last finding a home in Calicut. In order to save his life he had pretended to become a Mohammedan, and had adopted the customs of a Moor; but at heart, he said, he was still a Christian.

Joan begged his host to go with him next morning to the ships, where he would be sure of a hearty welcome from Vasco da Gama. The man, whose name was Monsayde, readily accepted the convict's invitation; and early in the morning, having taken leave of the Gozil (for Vasco da Gama had strictly enjoined upon Davane to omit no ceremony of politeness), the three went out in a boat to the "San Raphael."

As soon as Monsayde found himself on deck, he ran up to Vasco and Paulo da Gama, who were seated on the quarter-deck, and, making a profound bow, exclaimed in Spanish, —

"Good luck, sirs! good luck! Many rubies, many emeralds! You are bound to thank God for bringing you to this port; for here there is plenty of all sorts of spices, precious stones, and other riches."

Vasco's surprise at hearing him speak Spanish was as great as that of Joan had been; while the sailors and crossbow-men, who had gathered around, were so much affected at hearing the familiar tongue of their neighbors, the Spaniards, that some of them fairly wept for joy.

"Honored Castilian," said Vasco in welcome, "God give you health!" Before long, Monsayde was on the best possible terms with the captain and the Portuguese. Vasco made him sit on a stool by his side, and tell how he came to be in this remote country, and, dinner-time having arrived, invited him to dine, which he did, sitting at a table with Joan Nunez, while the captains ate at another near by.

Then Vasco da Gama told Monsayde about the voyage, and the objects for which he had come, and asked if he thought the Zamorin would prove friendly to him.

Monsayde listened as if he had something on his mind: he seemed troubled, and twitched about nervously on his seat. At last he broke out, speaking as if with an effort, and said, —

"Listen to me, captain; for I have something to confess. When I came on board this ship, I had it in my heart to betray you. I came as a spy for the Arabs, your enemies, and was going to reveal to them all that I heard and saw. But you have treated me so kindly, and God so smites me in my conscience, that I will truly be your faithful and devoted friend."

He went on to tell Vasco how the Arab merchants, jealous of the Portuguese, and fearful lest the arrival of the ships boded no good to their trade, had conspired to have the ships sent away; that they had bribed the Gozil and treasurer to aid them by setting the Zamorin against the Portuguese; and that they had promised Monsayde himself handsome gifts if he would come and pretend friendship for the strangers, make himself acquainted with their affairs, and betray them to the Arabs.

"It was with this bad purpose," Monsayde went on, "that I invited your men to my house, and that I came on board this ship. But now I pray you, captain, command me what to do, and you shall see that I am not false to you; though it is reasonable that you should not trust me, since I appear to you in the guise of a Moor among Moors."

Vasco da Gama, however, accepted his proffer of service, and, presenting him with some green cloth, told him that his reward would be much greater if he proved trustworthy.

It was then arranged that Monsayde should pretend to betray the Portuguese to the Moors; and, for this purpose, Vasco feigned to forbid him to come to the ships again, and sent him on shore.

Vasco da Gama, having considered what Monsayde had said, announced to Paulo and Coello, that, if the Zamorin invited him to visit him, he should boldly go and intrust himself in his hands. Against this the other captains warmly protested, and asked Vasco what would become of them if he should meet with foul play. They begged him to send some one else, who might represent that he was the captain, and so make terms with the Zamorin.

But Vasco da Gama replied, —

"My brother and my friend, when I embarked on this voyage, I gave up my life and soul to bring it, if God mercifully pleased, to a successful end. And I tell you, that if I were now back within the bar of Lisbon, having failed, I would take my life with my own hands rather than appear discomfited before the king. So, you see, I value my life little; and I should be despicable indeed if I were to put a man in my place to do that which I myself ought to do. I shall go on shore, fearing nothing, but trusting in God. And if, my brother, any disaster befall me, I pray you to go on, and fill these ships with cargoes; or, at least, to return to Portugal, and tell the king what has happened. If the weather is foul, then do you go along the coast, and get such drugs as you can find; but seize nothing forcibly, else the saying of the Arabs, that we are robbers, will become true."

Paulo, seeing that his valiant brother would not be turned from his purpose, promised, that, in case Vasco met with disaster, he would in all things follow his commands.

But the Zamorin, who was all the time being worked upon by the jealous Arabs, was not yet ready to receive the captain. Accordingly, he sent a message, that Vasco should despatch to him some one in whom he had confidence, to explain what the Portuguese wanted, and in what way they desired to make peace. Whereupon Vasco lost no time in confiding this task to his trusty friend Nicolas Coello, enjoining on him to tell the Zamorin that what the Portuguese wished was liberty to trade freely, and on equal terms with others, in Calicut; that they desired to go on shore, and buy and sell goods, without being molested, and to be provided with boats for carrying the goods to and fro.

He further ordered Coello to tell the Zamorin, that if these privileges were granted, and hostages were sent on board, the captain himself would go on shore and conclude a peace with him.

Coello, arrayed in a handsome suit, and attended by twelve sturdy Portuguese, proceeded in boats to the town, and was soon conducted with much ceremony to the palace. At the palace-gate he saw a number of seats made of mounds of earth, ranged around; and on one of these, which was covered with a mat, sat the Gozil, waiting to receive him; while just behind was a body of native soldiers, or Nairs, who formed the Gozil's body-guard.

It was now after sundown; and, while Coello was waiting somewhat impatiently to see the Zamorin, a message came from him that he was busy, and could not receive Coello till the next morning.

This made Coello angry, and at first he insisted on returning to the ships that night; but he was at last persuaded by the Gozil to remain in the town, at the house of a Christian, over night. At this house Coello was well entertained; for they feasted him on rice, chickens, and figs, and gave him and his comrades large, comfortable mats upon which to sleep.

Just before retiring, Coello happened to step outside the door a moment, when, to his surprise, he found the Spaniard Monsayde lurking in the shadow of the house. Monsayde put his finger on his lips, as if to warn the other not to speak aloud; and, drawing him aside, whispered, —

"I have been on the watch ever since you came ashore, and have been hiding here to get a chance to speak to you. They are trying to make you lose your temper, and rouse your anger, by delaying your interview with the Zamorin. So you must dissemble, and take every thing leisurely, and pretend you are in no hurry at all. If you get angry, they will take advantage of it to quarrel with you."

So saying, the faithful Monsayde crept away into the darkness. The next morning Coello took every thing easily, and appeared to care little how long the Zamorin made him wait. On being escorted to the palace, he was met by the treasurer, who told him that the Zamorin was unwell, and that he would receive the message Coello had to deliver; but Coello refused to deliver it to any one but the monarch himself.

Finding the Portuguese obstinate, the Zamorin at last ordered that he should be ushered into his presence. Coello found him in a small, dimly-lit chamber, seated on a low lounge, on which was spread a white cloth. Near him stood a Brahmin, or native priest.

Coello observed the Zamorin with much curiosity. He was a tall man, and very dark, — much darker than most of his subjects. His broad breast and shoulders were quite bare, neither did he wear any garment whatever above the waist. From the waist to the knees he was covered with a sort of white skirt. But, if his garments were plain, the jewels that he wore fairly dazzled Coello's eyes with their brilliancy. On one arm, above the elbow, he had a bracelet set with enormous rubies: from this hung a pendant, in which shone a very large, glittering diamond. Around his neck was a necklace of pearls as large as hazel-nuts, and also a gold chain set with pearls and rubies. The Zamorin's hair, which was long and very black, was gathered in a knot on the top of his head, and around this knot was a string of pearls; while from his ears hung two enormous gold rings.

Coello bowed low to the Zamorin, and then stood in silence. The priest asked Davane, who was by, why he did not speak; to which Davane replied that he could not speak until the Zamorin commanded it.

Then the Zámorin told him to give his message, which he did through the priest and Davane, who acted as interpteters.

Coello was then dismissed, and told to wait outside the palace-gate for the Zamorin's reply. Ere long the Brahmin priest came out, holding a dry palm-leaf, on which Coello observed some rude marks and strokes. The priest solemnly took a string, which he wore round his neck, between his thumbs, and in this posture swore that the Zamorin had put his signature upon the leaf, which proved to be a decree granting the Portuguese the right to trade in Calicut as they desired.

Davane whispered to Coello to take the leaf as if it were a very sacred thing, make a low bow, kiss the leaf, place it on his head, and then in his bosom; all of which Coello did with a very sober face.

It was now time to return to the "San Raphael." As Coello was making his way to the shore, the Castilian Monsayde glided up to him in the crowd, slipped a paper into his hand, and hastened off without a word. On it was written some words in Spanish, to the effect that the captain should accept the royal decree, send some merchandise ashore to exchange for other goods every day, and appoint a factor, or trading-agent, to remain on land, and take charge of the sales and purchases.

Coello's return, and the result of his errand to the Zamorin, gave Vasco da Gama profound satisfaction; and so well pleased was he, that he ordered the flags to be run up the masts, the trumpets to be sounded, and the guns to be fired off; the discharge of the latter causing much commotion among the people on shore.

Vasco da Gama lost no time in availing himself of the Zamorin's permission to trade, and in taking the advice secretly sent to him by the worthy Monsayde.

He selected a shrewd man, named Diego Diaz, who had been employed in King Manuel's household, as factor to conduct the trade with the people of Calicut; and ordered Nunez, Davane, and the Melinda pilot, to accompany him on land, select a good store, and begin business.

Anxious to propitiate the Zamorin in all things, Vasco said to Diaz as he was going away, —

"Do not seek to obtain more goods than are willingly offered you. See to it that you pay cheerfully whatever is asked, as if you were making a good bargain; and do not try to cheapen the goods. Appear to be well pleased and satisfied with every thing."

Having received this cautious advice, Diaz and the others went ashore. The Zamorin's treasurer, who, though bribed by the Arabs, was afraid to show hostility to the Portuguese lest he should arouse the Zamorin's anger, had already procured them a large warehouse with two spacious rooms on the quay, and had provided it with benches. Here Diaz and his companions took up their quarters, and prepared to begin trading. Vasco sent on shore a chest of coral, another of vermilion, a barrel of quicksilver, a quantity of copper, some amber, and money; and, to furnish the warehouse, a table covered with green cloth, and a wooden balance and weights for measuring. He also despatched a clerk to aid Diaz in keeping his accounts.

A large crowd of natives soon surrounded the warehouse; and it was with difficulty that they were kept from crowding in. The Gozil and treasurer went in and settled with Diaz the prices of the drugs which he wished to purchase. The prices of the goods which the ships had brought, and which were to be exchanged, were also agreed upon.

Then a lively scene presented itself in front of the warehouse. Huge bags of pepper and other spices and drugs were brought, weighed, and put on board the skiffs waiting at the quay, which carried them out to the "San Raphael" and "San Gabriel." Meanwhile, lines of swarthy natives were busy carrying into the town the coral and vermilion which Diaz had exchanged for the spices. Diaz took care always to give a little more than full weight, so that the Zamorin's officers should have no cause of complaint. He did not forget to slip some presents into their hands; and presented each of them with a handsome red cap and a fine steel knife, with which they were delighted. The next day Vasco da Gama sent more goods and money on shore, and the trade went on at the warehouse more briskly than ever. The Zamorin, finding that the Portuguese were lavish, and paid high prices for the drugs, was eager to keep the trade going, and told his officers to offer Diaz all the kinds of goods there were in the city; and Diaz bought a variety of articles, among others some planks and rafters, some ginger, cinnamon, and provisions.

On board the ships the men were busy receiving and storing away the cargoes. It was necessary to stow the pepper at the bottom of the hold; and the rafters and planks were used for making compartments, so that the goods might be stowed separately. These compartments were pitched so as to make them tight, and lined with heavy matting.

The treasurer, finding that Diaz took whatever was offered him, and paid well for it, brought some old and worthless cinnamon; and this, too, Diaz took and paid for, though he saw it was bad; thus obeying Vasco da Gama's command.

As this lively trade went on, the Arab merchants became more and more jealous of the newcomers, and redoubled their efforts to poison the Zamorin's mind against them. This was not easy to do, as the Zamorin, who was greedy of riches, was delighted with the gains he was making from the Portuguese.

The Arabs at last persuaded the Gozil to go to the Zamorin and tell him that it was evident the Portuguese had not come to trade, since they bought every thing, good and bad, that was offered to them, and paid foolishly high prices for worthless goods; but that they pretended to be merchants, so as to spy out the state of things at Calicut, and to come afterwards as marauders. They also begged him to advise the Zamorin to summon the captain, and receive his embassy, before permitting the trade to go on.

The Zamorin, covetous as he was, was struck by what the Gozil, prompted by the Arabs, said. Besides, he heard that Vasco da Gama had some rich presents for him, which he was going to bring when he came ashore; and the Zamorin was eager to obtain them.

So it was resolved that Vasco da Gama should be summoned to deliver his messages from the King of Portugal in person at the palace.

CHAPTER XVI.

VASCO DA GAMA VISITS THE ZAMORIN.

BESIDES his palace at Calicut, the Zamorin had a country-seat several miles out of the city. Instigated by the Gozil, who, in his turn, had been prompted by the Arab merchants, he resolved that he would resort to this country-seat, and receive Vasco da Gama there. His object was to get Vasco completely in his power, and if he thought best, after seeing him, to hold him prisoner.

Meanwhile he sent a Nair out to the "San Raphael" to apprise Vasco that the Zamorin expected him on the following day.

The faithful Spaniard, Monsayde, who had devoted himself heart and soul to the Portuguese, and had learned the Zamorin's design, made haste to warn the captain of it. The device he used to send him word, and at the same time not arouse the suspicions of the native officers, was a curious one.

Dressing himself up in tatters and rags, as soon as night came on he went along the quay, begging in a piteous voice, and soon reached the warehouse. Diaz was standing at the door. Monsayde made him a rapid and significant sign: whereupon the factor took him inside. Monsayde then told him to be sure and warn Vasco da Gama to insist on having hostages before he came ashore; and, having given this warning, the worthy fellow went out and proceeded on his way, begging as before.

Diaz found means to get word to Vasco; and the next day he demanded hostages of the Zamorin. Three Nairs were at once sent out to the "San Raphael," one of whom was a nephew of the Gozil. These were to be hostages for Vasco's safety; and the Gozil, who did not know what might happen, was somewhat fearful lest his nephew should come to harm. The three hostages went on board, dressed in handsome cloths, and wearing bracelets, ear-rings, and large shields and swords. Vasco da Gama now made his preparations to go on shore, and pay his long-promised visit to the swarthy sovereign of Calicut. He ordered the presents to be got ready, and twelve picked men to put on their best apparel so as to accompany him to the court in due state. The presents intended for the Zamorin were rich and curious. Among them were red cloths and velvets, a piece of yellow satin, a chair covered with rich brocade and ornamented with shining silver nails, two cushions of red satin with gold-thread tassels dangling at the ends, a chased and gilded hand-basin and ewer, a large and richly gilded mirror, fifty scarlet caps with crimson twisted silk buttons and tassels, and fifty sheaths of Flemish knives with ivory handles. These things were all carefully wrapped in fine napkins, and stowed in the boats which were to attend Vasco to the shore. Surely such presents were handsome enough to satisfy the greed of the most covetous of kings.

Just as Vasco was about to embark, he received a warning from Monsayde that the Zamorin had indeed gone off to his country-seat. This made Vasco angry, and he at once sent word to the Gozil that he would not come ashore until the Zamorin had returned to his palace again.

The Zamorin then reluctantly returned to Calicut, and now at last avowed his readiness to receive Vasco at the palace.

As the boat bearing Vasco da Gama, his twelve guards, and the presents, pushed out from the "San Gabriel," it presented a gay and novel sight to the concourse of natives who crowded the quays. Flags and streamers fluttered at the bow and stern; cannon peeped over the sides; trumpets were blown; and the rich apparel of the captain and his companions shone brilliantly in the sunlight.

On landing, Vasco da Gama repaired to the warehouse; and there, shut out from the gaze of the immense throng, he dressed himself so as to appear worthily before the Zamorin. He put on a short tunic of blue satin and a handsome enamel collar. Around his waist he tied a rich sash, in which was a gold-handled dagger. Over all he wore a cloak of yellow satin lined with brocade, which reached to the earth. On his head he placed a blue velvet cap, adorned with a long white feather; and his feet were covered with white buskins.

Thus arrayed, Vasco da Gama went out of the

warehouse, in front of which a procession was formed to go to the palace. By the captain's side walked a handsome young page dressed in red satin. In front of him marched his twelve guards, one behind the other, bearing the various presents; the one who carried the chair going first. On either side of the Portuguese proceeded a body of two hundred Nairs in military costume, commanded by the Catual, or captain of the Zamorin's guard. This Catual was destined to play a prominent part in the events which followed. In advance of the procession marched several Portuguese trumpeters, blowing their trumpets with all their might; while, from the Portuguese boats moored off the quay, cannon were fired as the company set out. The crowd was so great along the route, that it was with difficulty that the Nairs could keep it from pressing upon Vasco da Gama and his men.

The Catual first conducted them to the principal pagoda, or temple, of the city. Vasco found this to be a large building of freestone, vaulted with brick. Entering, he was met by the priests, who took a sprinkler, and showered some holy water over the visitors. Then they handed them some powdered sandal-wood to throw upon their heads. About the temple Vasco observed many strange and hideous images; and in a niche he saw a figure, which seemed so much like the figures of the Virgin often seen in European churches, that Vasco imagined that the temple might be a Christian one. One of his companions, pointing to the hideous images on the walls, exclaimed, "If this be the devil, I worship God;" which made Vasco smile.

The procession setting out again, the crowd soon became so dense, that they had to take refuge for a while in a house on the way till the streets were cleared. A large body of native troops now joined them, and the *cortége* set forth again. As Vasco walked along, and saw not only the streets, but the doors, windows, and roofs, occupied by a closely-packed mass of swarthy spectators, he exclaimed, "They little think, in Portugal, with what honor we are received here!"

It was late in the afternoon when the procession reached the royal palace. Vasco found this to be a large and really handsome edifice, surrounded by pleasant copses of trees, and gardens brilliant with flowers and odoriferous plants, and adorned with fountains.

At the palace-gate a group of noblemen, richly attired, waited to receive the Portuguese captain, and to conduct him to the Zamorin's presence. At their head was a little old man, who proved to be the chief priest, and who warmly embraced Vasco da Gama. This priest then led them, first, into a large square in front of the palace; and then, under arches, through four spacious courts, each court being guarded by companies of Nairs.

At last they came to a large hall, around which were ranged rows of benches in a semicircle. A green carpet covered the floor, and the walls were hung with rich silks.

The Zamorin sat in a kind of balcony, on a sofa covered with white silk and gold-cloth: a heavy canopy hung above him. On his head he wore a sort of crown, on which glittered diamonds and rubies; and the rest of his dress was the same as that in which Coello had seen him.

Just by the Zamorin was a table, or stand, upon which was a gold basin. This contained betel,— a curious compound composed of the juice of a certain leaf, quicklime, salt, and other substances. This betel, as we have seen, was chewed by the

Indians, and had the effect of making the gums and mouth very red, and the breath sweet.

A page, holding a broad red shield ornamented with jewels, stood on the right of the Zamorin: on the left was another page, who held a large gold cup. A priest just behind the monarch ever and anon handed him some betel: this he would chew leisurely, and then spit it into the cup which the page held out to him. As he did this, his courtiers held their hands to their mouths, that their breaths might not reach the Zamorin.

Vasco advanced up the hall; and when he came in front of the Zamorin he bowed low three times, and lifted his arms towards the ceiling. The Zamorin pointed to a seat by his side, and made signs that Vasco should sit there: at the same time the Nairs conducted the other Portuguese to the benches on either side.

When the company were all seated, the Zamorin's servants brought some water in basins, and offered them to the Portuguese for washing their hands. Then figs and other fruit were brought to them. As they ate, the Zamorin watched them, and seemed very much amused at their manner of taking food. The fruit made the

Portuguese thirsty, and they asked for some water to drink: this was brought in ewers. They were told that they must not touch the ewers with their lips, but pour the water into their mouths, holding the ewers above. As they did so, some of the Portuguese choked and sputtered with the water, and others spilt it over their clothes and faces: this made the Zamorin roar with laughter, and slap his knees in great delight. Then the presents which Vasco had brought were laid at the feet of the dusky monarch, who — as each rich cloth made its appearance, the ewers and basins, the mirror, and the chair — gazed at them with greedy pleasure. Vasco, through the interpreters, begged him to sit in the chair, which the Zamorin did with great good nature.

Turning to Vasco, he asked him to tell the courtiers what his purpose was in coming to Calicut; but this Vasco refused to do, saying that he was ordered to speak only to the sovereign himself. The Zamorin accordingly led the way to an inner chamber, followed by Vasco, one or two of the highest nobles, and Nunez, Davane, and the old priest, who were to act as interpreters.

Vasco da Gama, when they were seated, addressed the Zamorin in these words: —

"Sire," he began, "you are great and powerful among the rulers of India, and all of them are under your feet. The King of Portugal has heard of your grandeur, and has longed to obtain your friendship and good will. He desires to send his ships hither with merchandise, to trade with your people, and buy pepper and drugs. He therefore despatched me with the presents which you see before you, and by God's mercy I have come safely hither; and if you, sire, give us welcome, other ships will come, when we return with our story of your goodness, and Calicut will flourish more than ever before with the trade which will spring up between us."

So saying, Vasco da Gama produced a letter, which he said came from King Manuel, kissed it, and placed it on his eyes, and, kneeling before the Zamorin, gave it to him.

The Zamorin received it graciously, put it against his breast as a token of respect, opened and looked at it, and handed it to his treasurer to be translated.

Then, addressing Vasco da Gama, he said, —

"You shall have whatever goods you wish to put on board, and may send your people into the town to amuse themselves, and they shall not be molested. I will read the letter, and answer it."

The Zamorin then questioned Vasco da Gama about his voyage, and the mishaps he had had, and asked him many things about Portugal. How far was it from India? Over what possessions did King Manuel rule? What were the products of the country? How many ships were there? and how large was the army?

Vasco replied to all his questions, and said to the Zamorin, —

"King Manuel has sent me out with the ships to discover the way to India, and to make peace with your Majesty. He commanded me not to return until I had done so. I fear, that, if I should return without having obeyed his commands, he would surely order my head to be cut off."

It was now almost dark; and the Zamorin dismissed the Portuguese, ordering that an escort should be provided for them. When Vasco da Gama and his companions emerged into the street, they found that it was raining hard, and all their fine dresses were likely to be spoiled. Nunez told some of the men to take the captain on their backs, and so carry him across the city; but Vasco would not listen to this. Then the Catual (captain of the Zamorin's guard) procured a horse; but, as there was no saddle, Vasco refused to mount him, and continued to go on foot through the rain.

When he got to the warehouse he was dripping wet, and he hastened to change his rich apparel (which was nearly spoiled by the rain) for a suit of plainer clothing. He then sat down and wrote and sent off a letter to his brother Paulo, giving him an account of his interview with the Zamorin, and his adventures in Calicut.

He slept that night at the warehouse; for he expected to be summoned soon again to the Zamorin to hear his response to the letter.

The next day he received a gratifying token of the potentate's good will. The treasurer came to the warehouse with some fine stuffs embroidered with gold, a large porcelain jar filled with musk, and a number of other curious articles, which he presented to Vasco in the Zamorin's name.

Meanwhile he announced that he had orders to make the warehouse more convenient for the Portuguese, and at once set some laborers to work building a spacious shed near by. When the shed — which was a rude affair, and took but a short time to put up — was finished, the treasurer had benches placed within it, where the native merchants might come and sit, and barter with the Portuguese.

The trading between the strangers and natives now went on more actively than ever, and Vasco da Gama watched the exchange of merchandise with much curiosity and satisfaction. The goods were weighed and bartered during the day, and the payments were made at nightfall. In the evening the spices and drugs were conveyed by the boats to the ships. Finding how much influence the Gozil and the treasurer had at court, and knowing the efforts of the Arabs to make these officers hostile to him, Vasco da Gama sent each of them some presents of satin cloth, knives, caps, and strings and branches of coral. Unfortunately, he gave more to the treasurer than to the Gozil: this made the latter jealous and angry, and all the more disposed to listen to the Arabs.

The Arabs were very much alarmed when they saw with what favor, in spite of all their efforts the Zamorin received the Portuguese, and the liberty which he gave them to trade in the city. They feared lest they should lose their own business altogether, and they redoubled their exertions to create enmity against the new-comers.

They lavished more presents on the Gozil; and, finding that the captain of the guard was intrusted by the Zamorin with the duty of attending and protecting Vasco da Gama and his retinue, they secretly went to him also, and gave him a large sum of money. They urged him to provoke the Portuguese in some way, so that they should get angry, and do something for which the Zamorin would order them all to be killed, and the ships to be seized.

The captain of the guard happened to be poorer, and therefore more greedy of money, than the other officers; and so he lent a very favorable ear to the promptings of the Arab merchants. He at last gave his consent to join in their plots, and prepared to put into execution a design which he formed. He was afraid to use any open violence towards the Portuguese, lest the Zamorin should punish him with the loss of his head; but he craftily devised a plan by which he hoped to entrap Vasco da Gama into some imprudent act which would give an excuse for doing him an ill turn.

A day or two after Vasco's visit to the palace the captain of the guard came to the warehouse borne in a litter, and told him that the Zamorin was about to go to his country palace, and that he desired Vasco to come and see him before he went. The Zamorin had really sent no such message, but was ignorant of what was going on.

Vasco da Gama, though cautious and on his guard, did not suspect any foul play. Believing that the Zamorin had sent for him, he told the captain of the guard that he would soon be ready to go with him.

Meanwhile the captain of the guard had taken good care that no one should tell the Zamorin what was taking place. He placed some of his guards at the palace-gates to watch all who went in and came out; and would not even allow the Gozil and the treasurer, whom he suspected of treachery, to go in to the Zamorin.

Before repairing, as he supposed, to the palace, Vasco da Gama gave instructions to Nunez about the trading, and told him to take whatever merchandise was brought to him, whether good or bad, and to pay what the natives asked for it, without question. Then he put on a red satin tunic, with a scarlet gown over it, and a red cloth cap upon his head. He chose eight Portuguese to attend him: these were dressed in woollen jackets, and had stout sticks, instead of swords, for arms.

The captain of the guard ordered a very handsome litter, made of silk ornamented with a good deal of fringe and embroidery, and supplied with a soft mattress, to be brought. When all was ready, Vasco da Gama got into the litter, and reclined on the mattress, and in this manner was borne away from the warehouse.

CHAPTER XVII.

VASCO DA GAMA A PRISONER.

JUST as they were setting out in the litters, Joan Nunez felt some one plucking at his sleeve. On turning round, he saw the Spaniard Monsayde, disguised. He put his finger on his lips, and whispered, —

"Endure what is coming, and be silent."

Then he slipped hurriedly away among the crowd. Nunez, as soon as he had a chance, told Vasco da Gama what Monsayde had said.

The afternoon was far spent; yet the captain of the guard, as he led the company through the long, low streets, seemed to be in no haste. They made many turnings, and were so long on their way, that Vasco da Gama began to suspect foul play. His suspicions were ere long amply verified. They kept going from street to street until the afternoon deepened into twilight, and twilight into night.

Finally the captain of the guard stopped before a row of rather large houses in an obscure street, dismounted from his litter, and, changing his tone suddenly, told Vasco da Gama roughly to get down also. At first, Vasco was terribly angry. He glanced around at his men, and at the troop of Nairs who had escorted them. He saw, that, in a struggle, his Portuguese would stand no chance; and reflected, that, even if he should succeed in overcoming the captain of the guard's men, he could not hope, through the strange city, and in utter ignorance in what part of it he was, to reach the ships in safety. He remembered, too, Monsayde's advice, and, seeing that prudence was the better part of valor, repressed his anger, and quietly submitted to the captain of the guard's insolence.

Vasco and his companions were conducted through the large houses into an inner court, where there was a smaller house. Here they were left to themselves, the captain of the guard taking good care to leave a sufficient number of Nairs on guard.

Vasco da Gama now had ample time to reflect on his situation. What did this mean? Were they imprisoned by the Zamorin's order? or was he ignorant of it? Was it a plot of the Arabs, to which a heavy bribe had induced the captain of the guard to lend his aid? What were they going to do with him and his men? Here he was in a city of semi-barbarians, who might not scruple to take his life, and to pillage and burn the ships. Did they intend to kill him and the rest?

These questions passed rapidly through his mind, and filled him with alarm; yet he saw that it was useless either to attempt to escape secretly, or to openly resist the Nairs. He resolved that he would keep his temper, and be patient, in the faint hope that the adventure might turn out to be less serious than it now appeared.

On the floor of the building where they were confined were spread a number of coarse straw mats, the only furniture the house contained. The Portuguese sat down upon these, and, finding it impossible to sleep, kept talking the greater part of the night of the strange event that had befallen them. Meanwhile Vasco da Gama paced restlessly up and down the room, deep in

VASCO DA GAMA A PRISONER. Page 22

thought, and so agitated that he could take no rest. To add to their discomforts, the night was very hot, and the room in which they were imprisoned very close.

In the middle of the night some Nairs came in and deposited on the floor some boiled rice, with fig-leaves for plates, some boiled fish which was not very savory, and a large jar of water. Several of the Portuguese ate and drank, but others were too much agitated to be hungry; and Vasco da Gama did not touch the food.

The morning was far advanced before they attempted any thing to relieve their suspense. Then Vasco da Gama tried to send Joan Nunez out with a message to the captain of the guard; but the Nairs would not let him go. About noon some more rice and fish were brought in to them, and they were now hungry enough to eat the food. All that day and the next night they waited anxiously for some sign of what their fate was to be. Food was brought in to them as before; but they received no news of the captain of the guard, nor did they get any inkling of what he meant to do. Vasco's companions lost their patience at this long and mysterious imprisonment, and began to threaten violence against the Nairs: but he calmed them, and told them to put a good face upon the matter, as it was time enough to fight when the affair became desperate; and said that God would deliver them, if it so pleased him.

When they had been in the house two nights, some Nairs came in and told them that the captain of the guard had ordered them to be conveyed to another place. Following their sentinels, the Portuguese went out and walked through the streets, carefully guarded by a large number of native soldiers. Presently they reached the outskirts of the city, and soon found themselves going through a deep thicket, the sun blazing down upon them with a suffocating heat.

About noon they came to the bank of a small river. Here they saw two long Indian boats moored at the brink. The Nair, who seemed to be in command of the rest, ordered Vasco da Gama and three of his men, one of whom was Nunez, to get into the first boat; and the other five Portuguese were pushed into the second boat. Then the Nairs got in, and began to row the boats rapidly up the river. As they passed along, they saw large Indian villages on either bank, the inhabitants of which flocked out, and looked at them with much curiosity and amazement. Here and there the river ran between gloomy thickets; now and then broad sandy plains stretched away from the banks. The boat in which Vasco da Gama was soon left the other boat far behind; and once, when he looked round, he perceived that the latter was quite out of sight. He was angry at this; but the Nairs paid no attention to him, and rowed steadily on.

By and by they came to a small hamlet, where there were several low, thatched houses. The boat stopped near the bank, and waited while some rice was cooked. Neither Vasco nor his companions were allowed to land. The rice was handed to them; but Vasco was so irritated and amazed at his treatment, that he would not touch it.

The boat sped on, and did not stop again till darkness fell. Then the prisoners were taken ashore, and shut up in a small house for the night.

Very early in the morning, Vasco da Gama was suddenly awakened by a Nair, who told him that the captain of the guard had arrived, and wanted to see him. To put on his cloak and sally out took but a moment; but they would let none of his men accompany him, except an interpreter. As he went away, Vasco warned the Portuguese to be discreet, and say or do nothing, whatever happened. Meanwhile the other boat had come, and the Portuguese who had been brought in it were lodged in a hut close by that in which Vasco had passed the night.

He was led a short distance among the brush, and soon came to a narrow path, running through a dense, low thicket. Presently he reached an open place where were some more huts, into one of which he was conducted, and there shut up alone. Although indignant at this treatment, he could at least comfort himself with the thought that he was still alive. He had, indeed, escaped a great danger. The Arabs had tried to persuade the captain of the guard to kill him as he went through the lonely thicket; but the captain had refused to do so, fearing the Zamorin's anger.

Vasco passed a lonely and sleepless night in the solitude of his new prison, and was relieved, when, in the morning, he was at last led to the captain of the guard. The captain was sitting on a couch

When Vasco entered, he neither offered him a seat, nor spoke to him: a surly frown was on his dark face. In a moment or two Joan Nunez was brought in to interpret what was said.

The captain of the guard then spoke in an insolent tone, through Nunez, to Vasco da Gama.

"We have heard," he said, "from Mombaza, that you Portuguese are robbers, going about the seas plundering; and the Zamorin has ordered that your ships should be taken, and all of you kept prisoners till you confess the truth. Now, you had better tell me the truth, and I will go and relate it to the Zamorin."

"If you will conduct me to the Zamorin," replied Vasco, "I will tell him the truth; but I will not tell *you* any thing."

The captain of the guard got up in great anger, and cried out, —

"Why won't you tell it to me?"

Vasco remained silent.

The captain kept on asking questions; but Vasco did not open his lips. Then the enraged officer ordered the Nairs to take him away, and to shut him up in a house by himself. He next tried to get something out of Nunez: but this shrewd fellow evaded his questions; and he, too, was again imprisoned.

Finding that he could not make Vasco or any of the Portuguese angry (which he intended when he took them prisoners and brought them away), and fearing to do them any violence lest the Zamorin (who was ignorant of all these things, being away at his country-house) should order his head to be cut off, the captain of the guard was greatly puzzled what course to take.

At last he resolved that he would try to recover Vasco's good will, and get out of the scrape as best he could. He had obtained all the money from the Arabs that he could hope for; and his interest now was to shield himself from the Zamorin's anger.

The next day, therefore, he sent for Vasco, and told him that the Zamorin had made up his mind that all the merchandise on the ships should be sent ashore to the factory; and that then, in four days, he would allow him to take in his cargo of spices and drugs; after which, the ships should sail without delay.

Vasco replied, that he would obey the Zamorin's commands, but that, in order to do so, it was necessary to send a messenger to the ships. The captain of the guard then sent for the rest of the Portuguese to come to their captain: and, when they saw Vasco, they gathered around him, and shouted for joy; for they had been haunted with the fear that he might have been murdered.

But Vasco da Gama's troubles were not yet over. The captain of the guard conducted him back to the city, and lodged him on one of the quays, at some distance from the warehouse.

From this new prison Vasco was allowed to send a message to his brother Paulo. He apprised him of all that had happened, and that he was still a prisoner; told him to send the goods ashore; warned him to see that the hostages did not escape; and, if Paulo found that Vasco was not released, to order back Diaz the agent, and allow no one to go ashore.

He now attempted to get his release, and go to the "San Raphael;" but this the captain of the guard would not permit. Vasco subdued his anger as best he could, and this time sent a very different message to Paulo.

"Tell him," said he to the messenger, "that I do not think they intend to set me free, no matter how many goods are sent on shore; and beg him, for God's sake, if he sees they will not release me, to send the hostages ashòre, and then at once set sail. If they do not allow me to go when the hostages come, then let Paulo return at once to Portugal, and tell the king what has happened. For it is little matter if I am killed; but it is of great importance that the news of the discovery of India should be carried back to Portugal."

When Paulo received this message, he warmly declared that he would not go away without Vasco, but would risk his life, and that of all the men, in the attempt to deliver him, as they were all ready to die for their captain.

"Let the captain of the guard beware," said he; "for I will make war, and destroy every ship in the port."

Paulo ordered that no more goods should be sent ashore, and sent word to Vasco that he should remain to defend him.

The captain of the guard, angry that the goods were not sent (for he expected to get a share of them himself), thought it time to speak to the Zamorin, and, while concealing his harsh treatment of Vasco, to try and rouse his anger against him. He told the Zamorin that the Portuguese had not only refused to send any more goods on shore, but were threatening to burn the city and the ships. The Arab merchants added their persuasions to those of the captain of the guard; and their story so enraged the Zamorin, that he ordered that the goods at the warehouse should be seized, and that Vasco and his comrades should at once be put to death.

The captain of the guard was hurrying away joyfully to obey this command, when the chief priest, a venerable man, told him to stop.

Turning to the Zamorin, the priest said, —

"Sire, do not do this thing. Even if what the captain of the guard says is true, the Portuguese have as yet done no harm, but, like good people, have been very mild and peaceable. Do not execute your will until they show a disposition to do some injury."

This wise advice was adopted by the Zamorin, after a fierce debate with the Arabs.

Only one way to secure the release of Vasco da Gama remained to Paulo: this was to send the hostages on shore, and to trust to this magnanimous act, and to their persuasions with the Zamorin, to obtain Vasco's freedom.

The hostages, who had been kindly and gener ously treated by the Portuguese, willingly agreed to use every effort to accomplish this; and they were accordingly sent off in a boat, having received presents of red caps, knives, and satin cloths.

They hastened to the palace, and, kneeling before the Zamorin, revealed to him the whole story of Vasco's imprisonment, and the treatment he had received at the hands of the captain of the guard. They besought him to set Vasco free, and declared, that, if he did not, they would kill themselves, as they had staked their heads on the Zamorin's good faith. They begged him to reflect what dishonor and bad reputation he would incur if Vasco met with foul play, and assured him that the Portuguese meant no harm to him or the city.

The Zamorin was amazed and angry to hear of the captain of the guard's conduct, and at once resolved to make all the reparation in his power. Sending for Vasco da Gama, who was wholly in the dark, and did not know what was coming next, the Zamorin frankly begged his pardon for what had occurred, and declared that he would severely punish those who had been guilty of it. He told Vasco that he might go to his ship as soon as he pleased; and, as he spoke, he gave him a large jewel set with rubies and pearls in token of his regret and good will.

Vasco da Gama lost no time in taking advantage of his freedom. Attended by his Portuguese comrades and a large company of Nairs, he hastened to the quay, got into a boat, and set out for the "San Raphael." Just as the boat was pushing off the Spaniard Monsayde ran up and jumped into it, Vasco willingly consenting that he should go off to the ship with him. When Vasco appeared on deck, his brother rushed forward and fervently embraced him. The sailors gathered around him, and many of them wept for joy at beholding their beloved captain once more; and that night there was much feasting and merriment on board the ships.

Monsayde now took occasion to tell Vasco and Paulo the story of the captain of the guard's treachery, of the Zamorin's ignorance of his conduct, and of the hostility of the Arabs.

Vasco, much pleased with Monsayde's fidelity, overwhelmed him with presents, and gave him a paper, which recorded his testimony that the Spaniard was a sincere friend to the Portuguese, and a true Christian. The brothers now resolved to set sail without delay, lest other mishaps should befall them at Calicut. They had gained the objects for which they had come from their far-distant land,—the discovery of the way to India, and the possession of a cargo of drugs and spices; and there was no reason why they should tarry longer.

Monsayde went ashore, being bidden God speed by all the Portuguese, and delighted with Vasco's generosity and praise. The Zamorin, hearing of his arrival, sent for him to go to the palace. Monsayde told him that the ships were going away, and that they were terribly angry at the conduct of the captain of the guard and the Arabs.

While the ships were waiting for a favorable breeze, Vasco was surprised to see Monsayde return with a priest. They came with a message from the Zamorin, who repeated his regret for what had taken place, and apprised Vasco that the captain of the guard had been arrested, and would receive his deserts. He entreated him to return to Calicut, promising that he should have all the goods he wished.

Vasco returned a reply by Monsayde and the priest, to the effect that he accepted the Zamorin's expressions of regret, and would report his friendly words to King Manuel; but that he would surely avenge himself upon the treacherous Arabs, who had been the cause of all his trouble.

The next morning a fair wind sprang up; and taking a last look of the minarets, quays, and streets of Calicut, the Portuguese weighed anchor, and slowly sailed out into the open sea.

CHAPTER XVIII.

ALONG THE COAST OF INDIA.

SUMMER was gone, the cold and inclement summer of the East, which is like the winter of the West. It was late in October, or early in November, when the good crafts "San Raphael" and "San Gabriel" floated out of Calicut harbor. Vasco da Gama's voyage had already lasted a year and seven months; and many months more must elapse before his eyes would be again gladdened by the spires and domes of Lisbon, and he would reap the reward of his intrepidity and perseverance.

When the ships left Calicut, Vasco intended to sail directly for the African coast, and thence around the Cape of Good Hope home; but they no sooner found themselves in the open sea than they were struck by contrary winds, and were forced to proceed slowly along the coast of India. The trade-winds were still blowing steadily from the west; and, though the ships were not more than half laden, they were yet so worn, and had passed through so much stress of weather, that the pilots did not think it safe to venture in the face of the trade-winds.

They crept slowly northward along the coast, and one morning came again in sight of Cananor. It seems, that, during their stay at Calicut, the King of Cananor had kept himself informed of the doings of the Portuguese. As we have seen, his soothsayers had warned him that India would one day be conquered and ruled by Europeans, and had told him that these were the people meant by their prophecy: so he was eager, not only to show the Portuguese that he could be a better friend than the Zamorin, but to gain their good will, in case they came again to subdue the country.

As soon as the ships appeared off Cananor, therefore, the king sent out boats with messengers to implore the captain to visit him; at the same time offering him presents of jars of wood and water, figs, fowls, fish, and butter. He protested that he desired nothing so much as the friendship of the Portuguese.

Vasco da Gama was greatly pleased at this, and displayed his flags and fired his cannon in token of his good will. At first he hesitated about going ashore; but the king sent to him so many times, and urged him so earnestly, that at last he yielded.

In order that Vasco might not have the least suspicion or fear of foul play, the king ordered a long wooden bridge to be built out into the sea, at the end of which a small pavilion was erected. This bridge was made so narrow that two men could not walk on it abreast.

The king then repaired to the pavilion, attended by six or seven of his chief nobles; and Vasco and Paulo went to him in their boats, richly attired, and carrying presents with them. The king walked out upon the bridge to welcome them, and, on conducting them within the pavilion, made them sit down beside him and relate their adventures. He declared his anxiety to make peace and friendship with the King of Portugal, and offered them whatever goods they wished to complete the cargoes of the ships.

Their stay at Cananor, which continued for nearly three weeks, was full of pleasant incidents, and interchanges of friendly acts between the king and the captains. They gave him a splendid sword enamelled with gold, coral, silver, brass, and copper basins, and silks and cotton cloths; and he, in return, presented each of them with a large gold collar set with rare gems, and a heavy gold chain with a jewel hanging from it crusted with diamonds and rubies.

The ships here completed their cargoes; and the captain and crews feasted merrily every day with the abundance of good things which the king lavished upon them. He also gave Vasco da Gama a letter written on a gold leaf for King Manuel, affirming his faithful friendship for him, and his desire to, in all things, serve the Portuguese.

When they were about to depart from Cananor, the faithful Moor Davane, who intended to remain in India, took leave of Vasco da Gama and his men. They were much grieved to part with this good friend; for he had been of the greatest service on the voyage and at Calicut. Vasco da Gama gave him a large sum of money, overwhelmed him with presents, and wrote him a letter bearing witness to his fidelity and value.

When the Moor went away he was embraced and cheered by the men, and could not restrain his tears at parting from them.

Once more the ships set sail, directing their course westward towards Africa. They had not got more than fifty leagues away, however, when the wind fell, there came a dead calm, and they floated helpless on the waters. The trade-winds were still contrary; and it would be some weeks before they veered, and blew in the direction the ships wanted to go.

The pilot of the "San Raphael" said this to Vasco da Gama, and added that it would be well to return to land, and not imperil the ships by braving the bad weather.

"I am ashamed to return to land," replied Vasco; "for that is what people do who do not know how to navigate."

"We need not go back to Cananor," replied the pilot. "There is an island not far off the coast, where there is an abundance of wood and water, and a good shelter from the winds. Let us go and stay there until the trade-winds turn in our favor."

Vasco da Gama reluctantly assented to this proposal. He was anxious to find himself fairly homeward bound; yet he saw the prudence of the pilot's advice.

Taking advantage of a favorable breeze, the ships were once more directed towards the coast. Coming in sight of it, they ran along for some distance, and ere long came to the Island of Angediva, of which the pilot had spoken.

They soon found a sheltered bay, where the ships, when they lay at anchor, were almost completely hidden by an abrupt promontory from the sea beyond. Vasco lost no time in exploring the island, and discovered that it had only a single inhabitant,—an old Indian hermit, who lived alone in a hut, and subsisted on the rice which he got from the ships that passed by, and on the dried herbs which he found on the island.

The Portuguese went ashore, and roamed about their new sojourning place at will. They had not been there long before they found that many Moorish, Arab, and Indian ships passed near the island on their way up and down the coast; and that some of them were accustomed to touch there, and take in wood and water. At first, when these vessels rounded the point, and came suddenly upon the strange Portuguese caravels, they took fright, and sailed away as fast as they could.

One day the Melinda pilot took a boat and went out to a Moorish ship which was passing, and managed to catch up with it. Seeing that he was an African, she hove to, and took him on board. Then he explained who the Portuguese were, and for what purpose they had come into these parts; and assured the Moors that they were friendly, and intended no harm.

With this the Moors went ashore, and soon lost all their fear of the Portuguese. The news of their friendliness and generosity spread among the ports on the coast; and the ships that passed no longer hastened to take the offing, but came confidently into the bay for their wood and water. At the same time, they exchanged figs, rice, chickens, and cocoanuts, for the caps, knives, and cloths which the Portuguese had brought to trade with. Vasco hired some of these boats to catch and bring him fish, which he caused to be dried and salted, and so laid in ample provisions for his return-voyage; and a great rivalry sprang up among the Indians to see who should bring and sell their fish first.

The stay of the Portuguese at the Island of Angediva, however, was not wholly without its dangers. An event occurred which showed them the peril they risked in remaining off the Indian coast, and which nearly proved fatal to the expedition.

At Goa, a large place many leagues north of Calicut on the coast, there reigned a king named Sabayo, who, jealous of the Zamorin, and greedy for plunder, resolved to seize the Portuguese ships, and capture their merchandise and other valuable freight.

In the service of Sabayo was an old Jew, who had wandered thither from Spain, and who had proved so expert in naval warfare, that the king had made him admiral of his fleet. Sabayo chose this man to go with a large number of boats and men, well armed, to reconnoitre the Portuguese ships, and, if he could by stratagem, capture and bring them into the port of Goa.

The Jew set out, and arrived one night near Angediva, just around the point, where the Portuguese could not see his boats. He waited till it was quite dark; when, taking a boat with sails and oars, he swiftly rounded the point, and approached as near the ships as he thought was safe. He at once recognized them as Portuguese, having himself come from Spain. Satisfied with what he observed, he returned to his fleet, and waited till morning.

Meanwhile the fishermen whom Vasco da Gama had treated so generously had spied the Jew's boats concealed behind the point, and among the little islets that lay there; and knowing that they came from Goa, and suspecting that they had come for no good purpose, these fishermen hurried to the "San Raphael," and apprised Vasco da Gama of the arrival of the Goa boats, and of their suspicions. Vasco made them a handsome present for this friendly warning, and put himself on guard against the hostile designs of the Jew. The cannon were got ready, and a strict watch was set through the night. Early in the morning, a boat was seen rounding the point. It swiftly approached the "San Raphael." The Jew, who was seated in the stern, pretended to be passing by chance, and to espy the "San Raphael" by accident. He took in his sail, and, coming up within hearing, shouted out in Spanish, —

"God preserve the ships, the Christian captains, and the crews who sail with them!"

Vasco thought it best to dissemble, and so responded with a hearty greeting.

"Captains," continued the Jew, "give me a safe conduct, and I will come on board of your ships, and learn news of my country. I have been forty years a captive, and God has sent you hither, and I will tell you all you wish to know about these parts."

Vasco replied that he might safely come on board: whereupon the Jew climbed up the side of the "San Raphael," and stepped on deck. He was a tall old man, with long white hair, and a snowy beard which swept down over his broad breast. Vasco made him sit down and relate all that had happened to him, and how he came so far away from his own land. The old Jew answered willingly, meanwhile looking sharply around to see how many men there were on board, and what the chances were of capturing the ships.

While Vasco detained him in conversation, Paulo da Gama quietly sent word to Nicolas Coello to come over from the "San Gabriel" to board the Jew's boat, and seize his oarsmen. When Vasco saw that this was done, he arose suddenly, and ordered some sailors who were standing by to seize the old Jew, and bind him hand and foot.

The Jew was astounded to find himself in this predicament; and, appealing to Vasco, said piteously, —

"O sir, noble Christian, God protect me and you! I have trusted myself to your words; and here I am, bound hand and foot."

"Jew," replied Vasco, "you were treacherous when you asked for a safe conduct, and that shall not avail you."

Then they loaded his feet with irons; and his rowers, being brought on board, were carried bound below decks. Vasco then ordered that the Jew should be stripped and flogged; and told him, that, if he did not confess the truth, he would have hot fat dropped upon his naked flesh.

With this the Jew cried out in the midst of his pain, —

"O sir, I am worthy of death! But have pity on me and my white beard, and I will tell you the whole truth."

Vasco then commanded that he should be dressed; and the Jew related all that had happened, and told his real purpose in coming to Angediva.

"Now, Jew," said Vasco when he had concluded, "unless you deliver up all your boats and arms, I will have you flayed alive."

"Sir," returned he, "command me, and I will do it; for I am in your power."

Vasco da Gama now formed a shrewd plot for capturing all the Goa boats as they lay concealed around the point.

He waited till the shades of night had fallen before putting it into execution; then he ordered a number of boats to be got ready, manned with twenty men each, and supplied with swivel guns and powder.

The captain himself got into the Jew's boat, taking the Jew with him in irons, his hands being tied behind him. In this boat there were also several crossbow-men, and sailors to row it.

The little fleet set out after the moon had gone down, an hour or two before daybreak. Vasco's boat took the lead, the others following some yards astern. As they were rounding the point, Vasco turned to the Jew, who was moaning and bewailing his fate, and said in a low voice, —

"Now, when we reach your boats, you must speak to the men as if nothing was the matter, so that they may not be alarmed at our approach, and so prepare to resist us. If you fail to do this, your life shall be the penalty."

"Sir," replied the Jew, trembling, "I will try to save myself from death."

Presently they came so near that the Indians in the other boats heard them, and cried out, —

"Who is coming?"

The Jew replied, in as natural a voice as he could, —

"It is only I, friends: I am bringing some relatives with me."

This seemed to re-assure the Indians, who became quiet again. The Portuguese boats rowed up as quietly and rapidly as possible, and ere long surrounded the Indians. The gunners held their matches concealed, ready to touch off the cannon at the word of command.

All at once Vasco da Gama shouted in a loud voice the war-cry of the Portuguese, —

"*San Jago! San Jorgé!*"

His men gave a wild cry. The cannon boomed loud and sharp in the darkness, flashing a moment-

THE ATTACK ON THE GOA BOATS. Page 252.

ary and lurid light upon the scene; at the same time, the lighted powder-jars were thrown among the enemy. The boats took fire; and the Indians, many of whom were awakened from sleep by this terrible attack, plunged madly into the sea.

The Portuguese boarded the boats, but were too late to catch any of the Indians, who swam wildly for the shore, or hid themselves in the brush on the little islands near by. A number of those swimming were killed on the spot by the Portuguese cannon and the cross-bows: others were caught on the islands, and despatched without mercy. Then the boats were all taken in tow, and carried back to the "San Gabriel." In them were found stores of fish, rice, and cocoanuts, besides small cannon, javelins, swords, bucklers, and bows, with arrows made of cane, terminating in long, broad iron points.

The Portuguese stowed these away on the ships, and broke up the boats for wood. Vasco selected several of the Indians who had rowed the Jew's boat to do service at the pumps; and the rest were executed on deck, in presence of the crews and the old Jew. The latter, shivering with fright, and fearing that his turn would come next, begged piteously for his life. This Vasco granted him, ordering that he should be carried in irons below deck.

The trade-winds had now shifted, and were blowing briskly and steadily from the east. It only remained to complete the supplying of the ships with water and wood, and await the arrival of a favorable moment for departure.

The last days spent at Angediva were unmarred by any mishap; and, after the adventure with the Jew and his Indians from Goa, the fishermen and sailors who frequented the island treated the strangers with more respect and friendship than ever. Vasco found both his ships provided not only with a full cargo of spices and drugs, but with a great abundance of provisions, and even luxuries.

One morning when the sun shone bright, and a light breeze was blowing off shore, the "San Raphael" and "San Gabriel" swung out of the little bay which had so well sheltered them, and, skirting around the island, directed their prows westward toward Africa. Gradually the hills and coast of India faded from their view; and the Portuguese sang and prayed, as at last they felt themselves to be homeward bound.

CHAPTER XIX.

HOMEWARD BOUND.

VASCO DA GAMA, when he left Melinda, had promised the good king, that, on his return from India, he would pay him another visit: so the pilots directed the ships south-westward, hoping to strike near Melinda, on the African coast.

The voyage across the Indian Ocean was attended by few incidents worth relating. Although the trade-winds were now in their favor, blowing from the east, they did not escape some furious gales, and yet more annoying calms; and the sun's heat was sometimes intolerable. The ships had crossed from Melinda to Calicut in three weeks: it took them four weeks to make the African coast again on the homeward voyage.

Only two events occurred, however, to seriously mar the prosperous course of the journey. Scurvy again broke out among the men; and thirty poor fellows, falling victims to this horrible distemper, found a watery grave in that distant sea; while many others were rendered so helpless by it, that they were forced to lie in the cabin, and were useless for service about the ships.

When they were nearly half way across, the fresh water fell short; and all hands were put on half-allowance. This caused a great deal of dissatisfaction and grumbling; and soon the pilots began to demand that the ships should put back to Calicut. When Vasco da Gama would not listen to this, the pilots became mutinous; and Vasco was obliged to arrest them, put them in irons, and have them carried into the hold; after which he piloted the "San Raphael" himself.

At last the welcome coast of Africa came in sight, and the crews once more gave way to wild demonstrations of joy. It was about dusk when the dim outline of coast and mountains greeted their eyes. Vasco knew that this coast abounded in dangerous reefs and shoals, and so kept the ships well out to sea until morning should disclose their whereabouts, and the sun guide them clear of accident.

In the morning they stood towards land; and, running southward along the coast, they presently came opposite a large and prosperous-looking town. It had high walls around it, and on a height which arose from the middle of the town appeared a vast and lordly palace.

Vasco at first thought of putting in at this place; but learning that it was Magadoxo, a Moorish city, he abandoned his purpose, and passed it at a safe distance. He had had enough of Moorish treachery, and was resolved to avoid again putting himself in their power.

Some leagues farther on, they came to another town. While they were gazing at it, eight boats suddenly pushed out from shore towards the ships. They proved to be full of swarthy soldiers, whose intent evidently was to attack the Portuguese. But they were speedily disposed of; for the Portuguese fired several volleys of cannon-shot among them, which killed some, and effectually frightened the rest. The contrary wind would not permit the Portuguese to follow them, and the ships continued on their way.

It was on a bright morning in early January (1499) that Vasco da Gama once more caught sight of the imposing and friendly town of Melinda. The "San Raphael" and "San Gabriel" anchored in the roadstead; and Vasco ordered the streamers to be run up the masts, and the trumpets to be sounded. When the crews saw the familiar sights of Melinda, they cheered lustily.

A messenger was at once sent ashore to apprise the old king of the arrival of his Portuguese friends. He was soon followed by Vasco and Paulo da Gama in their boats. When they reached shore, they found the king on the beach waiting to receive them. He eagerly embraced the brothers, putting his arms around them affectionately, and made them sit down on either side of him.

The king questioned them about their journey, and renewed his promises of friendship and his expressions of good will. While they were talking, the two pilots whom the king had provided Gama to guide the ships to India came up and prostrated themselves before their sovereign, and kissed his feet. He asked them for an account of their adventures, which they gave him with great animation. On hearing about the Spanish Jew, the king expressed a desire to see him: whereupon the Jew was brought ashore, and presented to him.

After a long and pleasant interview, in the course of which Paulo da Gama begged the king to permit the two pilots to proceed to Portugal with them, which he readily granted, the captains returned to their ships.

They staid at Melinda twelve days. During this time, Vasco and Paulo went ashore and visited their royal friend every day, feasting with him till dusk, and exchanging costly presents. The ships were supplied with fresh water and provisions; and the crews had an opportunity to wander about the handsome town, buy curious knick-knacks for their wives and children (whom they hoped soon to see), and observe the bazaars and the dark-skinned natives.

When they were about to depart, the king sent a boatful of costly parting gifts. Among these were heavy neck-chains of gold set with gems, silver and ivory ornaments, jewelled rings, silks and gold-thread, for the King and Queen of Portugal, besides other presents for the captains and Nicolas Coello. In return, Vasco lavished so many presents on the king, that he exclaimed, —

"I am a poor man to be able to pay for all this."

There were coral and amber, vermilion and quicksilver, brocades, velvets, satins and damasks, mirrors, knives, caps, beads, gilt glasses, bars of copper, and a richly enamelled dagger which Vasco da Gama had long worn on his own person.

The ships stood out to sea on the morning of St. Sebastian's Day, and the friendly shores of Melinda soon vanished from the view. The next day the priests said mass on the decks; and in their prayers they made earnest supplications to God to preserve them, and bring them safely back to Portugal.

The Melinda pilots proved to be quite familiar with the coast, and often guided the ships safely by shoals which would have been dangerous had the Portuguese pilots alone been trusted. They warned Vasco to have the sails shortened as they passed Sofala, as there was a river there whence there sometimes issued violent squalls. The ships hove to, and sent boats ashore at several points along the coast. At one village they took in a large quantity of hens; and when they arrived at Zanzibar, finding the king of the island disposed to be friendly, and the people harmless, Vasco ordered the ships to cast anchor, and they remained there a week. During this time they took in provisions, exchanged presents with the king, had mass said on shore, and set up a pillar in commemoration of their visit.

Vasco took good care to sail wide of Mozambique, but anchored again at San Blas, where a new supply of water was obtained, and a number of seals caught, and salted down for provisions. At last, without any adverse incidents, the eyes of the Portuguese were once more blessed with the sight of the Cape of Good Hope; and as they turned it, and found themselves now running northward, full on the way home, and in familiar seas where they might reasonably hope to catch sight of European ships any day, their hearts were filled with joy, and, throwing themselves on deck, they uttered fervently their gratitude to God.

Soon after passing the cape, Vasco da Gama summoned the Portuguese pilots, who were still in irons on account of their rebellion while crossing the Indian Ocean, and said to them, —

"What do you men say of the great shame with

which you covered yourselves, when, from fear of the storm, you wished to seize upon me, and return to India?"

One of them replied, —

"Sir, we acted according to what we are: you acted according as you are. On a day of so much joy we pray that you will pardon us."

"I forgive you," said Vasco, "and I have no malice in my heart against you. But I have made a vow that I will take you in irons before the king, not to have you punished, but as a token of the perils of this voyage."

Vasco then had the presents of the King of Melinda brought on deck, and distributed them among the men, to their great joy; sending also an equal amount to the "San Gabriel," to be there divided in like manner.

The ships, instead of running along the coast where the continent of Africa bends, struck directly across towards the Cape Verde Islands; and, as they sailed, the "San Raphael" and "San Gabriel" were able to keep alongside each other, so that the men could speak from deck to deck. Even here the Melinda pilots were of great use; for, though they had never been on the Atlantic, they were able to take observations by the stars, and, with Vasco's charts, to steer a straight course. Now and then showers, calms, and contrary winds arose, and delayed the voyage; but happily they escaped the terrible storms which had assailed them on their way out.

They had left Melinda late in January, and it was not till the latter part of August that they once more came in sight of the Cape Verde Islands. Here a great sorrow overtook Vasco da Gama. His good and gentle brother Paulo had been taken sick soon after passing the Cape of Good Hope. At first, it seemed but a slight attack of cold: but, as the ships approached the islands, he grew worse and worse; and Vasco went on board the "San Gabriel" and tended him. When they put in at the Island of Terceira, Paulo had to be carried tenderly on shore; and the day after, to the intense grief of Vasco, he died in his arms. For his brother Paulo Vasco da Gama had the most devoted and faithful affection: and no wonder; for Paulo was a noble character, lovable, sweet-tempered, yet resolute when the occasion demanded it, and ready at all times to share every danger with his companions.

Paulo da Gama was buried in the little monastery of St. Francis, at Terceira; his grief-stricken brother following him to the grave, attended by all the Portuguese in deep mourning.

The ships were already so much worn by the long voyage, that it seemed doubtful whether they could reach Portugal. At Terceira Vasco found a colony of his countrymen; and these heartily assisted him to repair the caravels, and supply them with all things needed for their final journey. Vasco's crews had been dwindled by sickness and death to about fifty, and more sailors were added to them at Terceira.

Having made all these preparations, the "San Raphael" and "San Gabriel" set sail for Portugal. Vasco da Gama's heart was oppressed with sorrow at his brother's death; and the exultation which he might have felt to think that in a few days he would be received with enthusiastic rejoicings and the highest honors by his king and countrymen was now obscured by the gloom that overshadowed his heart.

CHAPTER XX.

WELCOME HOME.

KING MANUEL of Portugal had a country palace at Cintra, a few miles from Lisbon, cosily nestled at the foot of sloping and verdant hills, and in the midst of fruitful vineyards. Thither he was often wont to repair during the warm weather and at the harvest-time to get rid of the heat and dust of the city and the cares of business, his queen and a few favorite courtiers accompanying him to this pleasant retreat.

In the month of September, 1499, King Manuel was enjoying quiet and the pastimes of the country at Cintra. More than two years had elapsed since he had heard a word of Vasco da Gama and his expedition; and he had begun to fear that he should never see the brave captain and his caravels again. He had almost given up all hope that India would be discovered, and had even meditated sending out an expedition in search of Vasco and his companions.

One night, very late, the king was seated before a bounteous supper, feasting with his courtiers. The banqueting-hall was brilliantly lighted, and the table groaned with all the good things that the royal steward could procure and devise. The party were merry; and laughter often echoed through the hall at some sally by the jester, or witticism of a bright-witted courtier.

In the midst of the revel a loud knocking was suddenly heard. Presently a chamberlain entered, and announced to Don Manuel that a man had just arrived from the sea-coast, having come at full speed, who declared that he had most important news for the king. He begged to be admitted to an immediate audience. Don Manuel told the chamberlain to conduct the man into the banqueting-room.

The new-comer was a large, red-faced man, with the air of a seafarer. As he advanced and knelt before the king, his movements betrayed the roughness and awkwardness of a sailor.

"Who are you, and what do you want?" asked the king.

"Sire," replied the man, "my name is Arthur Rodriguez. I am the captain of a caravel trading between the Cape Verde Islands and Europe. I belong at Terceira, and have a wife there, and children. Sire, I have just come hither in all haste from Terceira, and this night landed at Cascaes, at the mouth of the Tagus, whence I have ridden on horseback without taking breath. I came," continued the man, still panting, "to tell your Majesty great news, glorious news."

"Ah!" exclaimed Don Manuel, rising, and going towards the man, while the courtiers flocked eagerly around. "What is this news?"

"I left Terceira four days ago, sire," Rodriguez went on; "and, as I was making from the island under sail, I passed two caravels which were entering port. They looked strange, and labored much in the water. Urged by curiosity, I brought my caravel near, shouted out, and asked who they were, and whence they came. They answered that they were just come from India, and that Vasco da Gama commanded them. So I hurried away, and made all sail for Lisbon, to be the first to tell this news to your Majesty. When I came off in a skiff, I learned that you were here."

At these words the king clapped his hands, and cried out joyfully; while the nobles manifested their delight by embracing each other, and gathering around Don Manuel to offer their congratulations.

"You shall be well rewarded for this," said he, when the first excitement of pleasure was over. "You shall be a gentleman of my household. If you have a son, he shall be a page of the chamber. And to-morrow my treasurer shall pay you a hundred crusados."

Rodriguez, with tears in his eyes, kissed the king's hand, and retired, hastening off to tell his friends of his good fortune.

Don Manuel's first thought was to repair to the chapel, recite his orisons, and to give thanks to God before the altar for the safe return of Vasco da Gama. Then he said to his nobles, —

"We must start for Lisbon at once, so as to be there when the gallant Vasco arrives. He will doubtless follow closely upon this Rodriguez, and should be received with all pomp and honor."

The king and his court set out about daybreak, and reached Lisbon in season for dinner. By this time another caravel had arrived from Terceira, hoping to be the first with the good news; and from the captain of this vessel the king heard of Paulo da Gama's death, and Vasco's intense grief at the event. Don Manuel lamented his affliction, and said,—

"I would that Vasco da Gama might have come to me with unalloyed pleasure; but, as it is, he must be consoled by such rewards and honors as his intrepid courage and great achievements deserve."

The king did not have to await long the arrival of the caravels; for one morning, a day or two after his return from Cintra, it was announced that they had entered the mouth of the river, and were fast approaching the bar below Lisbon. The news quickly spread from the palace to the city and the harbor; and all Lisbon turned out, and hurried in multitudes down to the quays. The harbor was full of ships and boats; and ere long they all appeared, gayly decked out with flags and streamers, while the sailors crowded on the decks in their Sunday suits. The people, also dressed in holiday attire, flocked through the narrow streets and across the broad squares; and the city hummed with excited voices, and shouts of joy.

On the principal quay was a large building with a balcony, over which hung a canopy: it was called the "House of the Mines." Hither the king, attended by the court, came; and seats were provided for the royal folks on the balcony.

Presently the booming of cannon was heard in the distance: it came nearer and nearer, and now was echoed by the cannon on the ships in the harbor. Then two caravels were seen, slowly floating in an open space which the vessels made for them towards the centre of the harbor. These, too, sent forth deafening volleys; and from their mastheads fluttered the royal standard and the flag of Portugal. They were the "San Raphael" and the "San Gabriel." Vasco da Gama could be seen by the nearest ships, standing on the quarter-deck of the "San Raphael," wearing a plumed cap, and waving his hands on this side and that. Below, on the main deck, the crossbow-men, sailors, and officers, with whom mingled the dark Melinda pilots in their Oriental costume, and the Jew from Goa with his sweeping white beard, huddled together at the sides of the ship, and gazed eagerly towards the dear and familiar shore.

What a thrilling scene it was! How the hearts of the weary wanderers must have bounded to behold each well-known object, — the spires of the churches, the well-remembered streets and squares, the easily recognized hills and cliffs, the spots where were their homes! And then how they must have strained their eyes towards the crowded quays, in the hope that they might make out the beloved forms of dear ones left so long ago behind! Soon, indeed, they would be locked in the embrace of parents, wives, and children, or would be bowed with grief at the news of the death of beloved relatives or friends.

The king sent out a great nobleman, named Vasconcelos, to greet Vasco, welcome him home, and beg him to come on shore; at the same time expressing his grief at the death of Paulo da Gama. Vasconcelos was followed by a crowd of Vasco's friends, who flocked on board to embrace him, and manifest their joy at getting him back again.

Vasco da Gama then dressed himself in a close-fitting silken tunic, a cloak, and a round velvet cap, and proceeded to the shore. Landing on the beach, he was greeted by the bishop, and a nobleman named the Count of Borba, who, after embracing him, offered to conduct him to the king. As Vasco went along towards the House of the Mines, the people observed that his beard had grown very long, and that his face was pale and sad. They shouted and cheered frantically as the hero passed between their ranks, and blessings were showered upon him on every hand.

When he ascended into the balcony, Don Manuel, as a mark of peculiar honor, rose from his chair to greet him. Vasco da Gama kneeled, and kissed the royal hand; but Don Manuel immediately raised him, and warmly embraced him.

"Sire," said Vasco, "all my hardships have now come to a happy end, since I am once more brought in presence of your Majesty, as I have always prayed."

"May your coming be fortunate," returned Don Manuel. "Your return fills me with pride and happiness; and, since God has been pleased to bring you back in safety, he has reserved you for the rewards which your heroism deserves. But, for my sake, be consoled for the death of your brother."

The king now descended, and mounted his horse, and with Vasco da Gama riding by his side, and the courtiers following in a dazzling group, repaired to the palace. Here he brought Vasco to his fair young queen, whose hand Vasco kissed; while she received him with graceful welcome.

Meanwhile a touching scene was being enacted on the quays. The sailors and other companions of Vasco da Gama on his voyage had come ashore, and were being overwhelmed with the joyfully tearful caresses of their families and friends. Their weather-beaten faces quivered with emotion as the dear wife, the bright young child, and aged mother, were fondly folded to their bosoms. Troops of old friends and cronies crowded around them and hugged them, and bore them away in triumph up the zigzag streets to their longed-for homes, where hearty feasts awaited them. Each man was a wonderful hero to his friends: he had braved unheard-of perils, and had seen such strange things and people as nobody had imagined existed on earth. That night many a group sat around the homely hearthstones of Lisbon, and listened to the marvellous stories of India and the East which the wayfarers told.

After Vasco da Gama had been presented to the queen, Don Manuel affectionately dismissed him, saying that doubtless he was weary, and needed rest; and told him to come to the palace next day, and recount his adventures more at length. An immense multitude of people accompanied Vasco from the palace to his own house, whither he retired for the night; but, before he could get to bed, many of his friends came to greet him, and congratulate him upon his safe return, and the great fame and honors that awaited him.

The next morning the city still wore a holiday look. The people, rejoiced at the return of the expedition, and proud of the glory and power which it seemed certain that Portugal would derive from the discovery of India, neglected their business, and made merry out of doors. Flags floated from the houses, and far and near you might have heard the strains of music celebrating the happy event.

Early in the morning, Vasco da Gama, surrounded as before by a great concourse of citizens, went to the palace as the king had commanded. Don Manuel was in his dressing-room, putting on his clothes before a mirror. When Vasco entered, the king came towards him with a smile of welcome, and extended his hands. Vasco kneeled; but the king, raising him up, said, —

"Rise, Don Vasco da Gama. You have rested but little."

The king called him "Don," and thus conferred on him that title, — a noble one, corresponding to "Lord."

Don Vasco again knelt, kissed the royal hand, and thanked the king for this high honor.

"I confer it upon you," said Don Manuel, "not only for yourself, but for the whole of your lineage."

The king then repaired to mass, having Don Vasco with him; and they stood together behind the curtain of the royal box, talking, as the service went on. Thence they repaired to the apartments of the queen; and Don Vasco sent for his faithful comrade, Nicolas Coello. When he had arrived, Don Vasco said to the king, —

"Sire, Nicolas Coello has been faithful and brave through all our perils and trials. I beg your Majesty to give him the rewards due to his merits."

"It shall all be, Don Vasco," returned the king, "as you wish."

Don Vasco now ordered the beautiful presents which had been sent by the Kings of Cananor and Melinda to be brought, and set before the royal pair. The chests were opened; and when the queen saw the glittering jewels and porcelain, and other gifts, she clapped her hands with delight.

Don Vasco then sat with the king and queen, and chief noblemen of the court, relating his many adventures, escapes, and triumphs; to which they all listened with rapt attention, hanging upon his lips as he described the thrilling scenes through which he and his companions had passed.

He told the king of the pilots whom he still kept in irons, and why he had thus punished them: whereupon Don Manuel said that he might order them to be executed, or set at liberty, as he pleased. Don Vasco also spoke of the Melinda pilots, and praised their intelligence and fidelity. The king sent a man to go about with them, and show them the city; and ordered that they should enjoy a bounteous hospitality; that they should be taken to the feasts and banquets, the bull-fights and other games; and that all the public edifices should be open to their inspection.

When Don Vasco returned to his house, he sent

for the pilots in irons, and, when they were brought, said to them, —

"I have kept my word to deliver you up in irons to the king. I have told him of your offences, and he has left the punishment of them to me. Now, I pardon you freely, because of the hardships you have undergone. Go in peace, and rest yourselves with your wives and children, with whom you will live with more pleasure and content than if you had gone back to India, flying from fear of the storms, and carrying me a prisoner, as you wished to do."

They threw themselves at his feet, weeping with gratitude, and exclaimed, "Sir, may you have your reward from God!"

The voyage of Vasco da Gama had lasted from March 25, 1497, to Sept. 18, 1499, — a period of about two years and six months. He had started with one hundred and fifty men, and returned with only one-third of that number. His frail little caravels had been new and stanch when he set out: when he got back they were worn and seemed old, and were no longer fit for such hard service.

It remained to settle up the accounts, to pay

the men, to distribute the cargo, and to dispense the rewards which had been so bravely won. The crossbow-men and sailors were generously paid in money, and were allowed, besides, to carry each ten pounds of spices home to their wives. The heirs of the dead sailors were paid their wages, and share of the goods; and each master and pilot received, besides his wages, half a quintal of every drug which the ships had brought. Nicolas Coello received a large sum of money, a quintal of the spices and drugs, a share of the presents, and was made a lord of the royal household. To Vasco da Gama, besides the noble title of "Don," King Manuel granted a yearly sum of two hundred ducats to spend in spices from India, which he should bring in free of duty, besides a pension of about a thousand dollars a year, which was then worth as much as ten thousand dollars is worth now. He gave him permission to wear the royal arms, and to adopt as his coat of arms two does, which in Portuguese are called *gamas*. He made him lord of the village of Sinis, in which Don Vasco was born; and gave him a large proportion of the precious cargoes he had brought from India.

King Manuel made offerings to various churches

and monasteries in token of his gratitude for the discovery of India; went with the queen in solemn procession to the cathedral, where the Bishop of Lisbon eloquently preached on the great voyage and discovery; and finally made a proclamation, in which he assumed the title of "Lord of the Conquest and Navigation of Ethiopia, Arabia, Persia, and the Indies."

Thus ended the famous first voyage of Don Vasco da Gama; and thus he was received, when, after so many dangers and adventures, he at last returned to his native Portugal. His fame rapidly spread through Portugal and all over Europe. He was hailed as the rival of Columbus, and the kings envied the good fortune of Don Manuel in having so valiant and persevering a navigator. Camoëns, the greatest of Portuguese poets, celebrated his heroic character and deeds in an epic poem, the "Lusiad," which still preserves his memory; and he became the pride and idol of his countrymen.

CHAPTER XXI.

CONCLUSION.

HAVING once tasted the delights of maritime adventure and the glories of discovery, Don Vasco da Gama was not content to rest indolently on his honors, and relapse into the dull monotony of a courtier's life. He longed for the excitements and perils of the sea, for the wild joy of its conquest, for the conflict with the tempest, and the struggle with the men of the East.

Events occurred, too, which roused his ambition anew, and inspired him to once more venture to the distant lands the route to which he had discovered. The spring after his return, another eminent Portuguese navigator, Alvarez Cabral, made the voyage to India, following, after passing the cape, almost exactly in Don Vasco's track.

He went with ten large ships and two caravels was driven on to the American coast, and discovered Brazil; visited Mozambique and Melinda; and made a long and rather troubled sojourn at Calicut, where the Zamorin, instigated by the jealous Moors, provoked him to destroy their ships in the harbor, bombard the town, and nearly reduce it to ruins. In the next year (1501) King Manuel sent Joan de Nueva with three ships to India, who, passing over Don Vasco's route, made some stay at Cochin, Calicut, and Cananor, and returned safely to Lisbon with all his ships.

These voyages filled Don Vasco da Gama with renewed eagerness to undertake another voyage to India; and this wish King Manuel could not deny him. Accordingly, on the 3d of March, 1502, two years and a half after his return from his first venture, Don Vasco set sail with a fleet of thirteen large ships and two caravels; and this fleet was soon followed by another of five ships, under the command of Stephen da Gama, Don Vasco's cousin, who joined him at Melinda.

This voyage was in many respects more successful than the first. Don Vasco succeeded in making friendly treaties with the formerly hostile

Kings of Sofala and Mozambique, and compelled the usurping King of Quiloa to pay tribute to Portugal. He paid a visit to his old friend, the King of Melinda, who received him joyfully, and feasted him on the fat of the land; and, reaching India in safety, he fought with and took many Arab ships, in revenge for their hostility to him on his former voyage.

He received the same treatment at Calicut as before; but now having a large force, after attempting in vain to secure a treaty of peace with the Zamorin, he bombarded the town, destroyed the royal palace, and made the place almost uninhabitable.

Don Vasco thence went to Cochin, the Rajah, or governor, of which town had already evinced to Cabral his desire to be on friendly terms with the Portuguese. Here he was able to take in full cargoes, and to leave some agents for the purposes of trade. While at Cochin, Don Vasco received a message from the Zamorin of Calicut, expressing his sorrow at what had passed, and begging him to return there. When he reached the harbor of Calicut, having come with only one ship (for he left the rest of the fleet at Cochin under his cousin Stephen's command), he found a large number of native vessels waiting to assail him. He made all haste to cut his cables, and return to Cochin.

The Zamorin was not content with this act of treachery. When he found he could not decoy the Portuguese ships to Calicut, he sent to the Rajah of Cochin, and tried to persuade him to make war upon them. The Rajah not only refused this, but, as Don Vasco was going away, warned him of the Zamorin's designs, and bade him beware of an attack.

The Rajah's fears were not groundless. Don Vasco sailed with his fleet from Cochin, but had not got far when a Moorish fleet of twenty-nine ships hove in sight, evidently with a hostile purpose. Don Vasco at once bore down upon them: three of his foremost ships closed with the enemy; and at the first onset the Moors leaped, panic-stricken, in large numbers into the sea. When the rest of the ships approached, the Moorish vessels made all haste to retreat. Two of them were captured, the goods they carried taken out, and the ships burned, the crews being shot without mercy. Besides these, the Portuguese killed three hundred Moors who were swimming about in the water.

Don Vasco repaired to Cananor, where he established a warehouse as he had done at Cochin, and left twenty Portuguese agents in charge of it, whom the king pledged himself to protect. In return, Don Vasco agreed that Portugal should defend the king from all assaults of his enemies. He left a squadron of ships under his cousin, Vincent Sodre, to cruise about the coast of India, aid their allies of Cochin and Cananor in case of necessity, and to make prizes of such Arab ships as they could.

The rest of the fleet sailed with full and valuable cargoes from Cananor for Portugal on the 20th of December, 1502, having been now absent a little more than eight months. The return-voyage was a stormy one, and in one tempest the fleet came near being destroyed; but they arrived safely at Cascaes, at the mouth of the Tagus, on the 1st of September, 1503.

King Manuel received Don Vasco and his companions with the same honor and hearty welcome as before, and made the heroic voyager Admiral of the Indies, and Lord of Vidigueyra.

After his return from this voyage, Don Vasco da Gama remained at home in Portugal for many long years. He had married, after his return from his first expedition, the fair Catharine de Atayde, daughter of the mayor of Alvor; and two sons had now blessed the happy union. A family of children soon grew up about him, and in course of time he found himself the father of six sturdy boys. These home attractions, the honor in which he was held at court, his wide-spread fame, his ample fortune, seem to have made him contented to remain quietly in Portugal.

Meanwhile King Manuel was resolved to take every advantage which the discovery of the route to India, and the relations of friendship with the African and Indian potentates, gave him. Portugal became the rival of the splendid republic of Venice in the attempt to obtain the control of the rich trade of the East; and King Manuel was forced to use every means in his power to prevent Venice from outwitting him.

Year after year, expeditions were sent out from Lisbon to Africa and India; the fleets carrying large bodies of soldiers, and beginning to make conquests along the coast where Don Vasco had met with so many adventures. In 1505, two years after Don Vasco's return, Francisco d'Almeyda set out for India with twenty-two ships; and the king, appointing him viceroy, charged him to effect permanent footholds on the Indian coast. D'Almeyda was a brave soldier and an expert captain. He built a fort at Cananor, and left one hundred and fifty soldiers there to guard it. Then he repaired to Onore, where he built another fort. He had many sea and land battles with the Moors and Arabs, but gained brilliant victories over them, and succeeded in laying a foundation for the powerful Portuguese empire in India, which lasted for centuries after.

Nor did he neglect the opposite African coast; for he erected forts and left garrisons at Quiloa, Mozambique, and Sofala.

D'Almeyda was succeeded as viceroy by the famous Alfonso d'Albuquerque in 1509. This really great man carried the Portuguese conquests in India to a far wider extent. He took the flourishing seaport of Goa, north of Cananor, and, passing around the continent of India, achieved a brilliant victory at Malacca; which place he fortified, and held in the name of his sovereign. He sailed into the Red Sea, making terrible havoc with the Arab war-ships and merchantmen; he took and built forts at Ormuz, and established the Portuguese flag at Diu. This able conqueror died in 1515 at Goa, having obtained for Portugal a wider dominion in the East than any European nation had ever held.

The Oriental trade which was thus procured rapidly made Portugal rich, and her power became the envy of her sister-nations. Her marts in India, Ceylon, and Malacca, enabled her to build up such a commerce as that even of Venice scarcely equalled. From thence she received the cloves of the Moluccas and the sandal-wood of Timor, the camphor of Borneo and the gold and silver of Luconia, the nutmegs and mace of Banda, and the gums, spices, and curious workmanship of Siam, China, and Japan.

These were all results of Don Vasco da Gama's perseverance and dauntless courage in achieving the discovery of a sea-path to India.

The time came when the old spirit of wandering and adventure again came over him. In 1524 he was not far from fifty-six years of age. He had grown-up sons, and his once thick brown hair and gracefully flowing beard were grizzled with the frosts of coming age. But he was not older than Columbus when he had risked the trackless Atlantic: he was still vigorous, stalwart, active, and warm-blooded. He longed to find himself again on the stormy deep, to see the dominion which his country had acquired in the India which he had found, and to have a share of the glory of the great events that were going forward.

Don Manuel was dead, but fortunately had been succeeded by a monarch equally devoted to the interests of Portugal in the East, in King John the Third. Having recalled the viceroy who was ruling in his name in India, he bethought him of Don Vasco da Gama, and offered him the office. Don Vasco eagerly accepted it, and forthwith set about the preparations for his departure. He was going in great splendor and state; for the post of viceroy was nothing less than a royal one in power and dignity.

Don Vasco little thought, as he sailed out of Lisbon harbor, that he should never behold his native land again. He went forth gayly, with high hopes of returning once more with new fame and greater honors. Under his command went fourteen ships, and these carried a force of three thousand well-armed soldiers. The admiral — for such he now was — lived on board the flagship with luxury and magnificence. He was served by major-domos, pages, and body-servants. He ate his meals on a table covered with rich brocade, from gilded and silver dishes. His wardrobe was splendid; and a body-guard of two hundred men, in gorgeous livery, attended him. Don Vasco's second and third sons, Estevan and Paulo, went with him to India. As the fleet, after losing three caravels on the African coast (with two of them all the men on board), approached the well-known shores of India, a strange and fright-inspiring event occurred. Of a sudden, and in a calm, the sea began to heave, and knock the ships about in an unaccountable way. They thought they were on shoals, but, on casting the leads, could find no bottom. The men could not stand on deck; and the huge chests were hurled violently from one side to the other. This upheaving of the sea continued for upwards of an hour. The water came boiling and bubbling furiously up; and the crews kept crying out for very terror. At last it became evident that an earthquake had taken place.

Don Vasca da Gama was received at Goa with great enthusiasm and honor. He was welcomed by the governor. Splendid feasts took place; and an immense concourse attended the new viceroy to the cathedral, where prayers were offered for his safe arrival. Thence he repaired to the fortress, where he took up his residence.

He now showed that he could be an able and vigorous governor as well as a brave soldier and an intrepid voyager. He was no sooner settled at Goa than he began to depose the Portuguese governors and captains, who were proved to have been guilty of oppression and corruption. The first of these who fell under his displeasure was Francisco Pereira, who commanded the fortress of Goa, who had been tyrannical, and had wrongfully obtained money of the people. Don Vasco forced him to return the money he had thus taken.

Don Vasco's rule as Viceroy of India was brief; for it lasted less than three months. During that time he was unceasingly active in reforming the offices and affairs of the many fortresses and settlements under his charge. He severely punished all officers who dishonestly made money out of their posts; and was very careful, in appointing new officers, to find out for himself whether they were fit to perform their duties. He regulated the trade of the various Indian ports, and forbade any vessel from going to and from them without his written permission. He visited various forts and settlements, among them Cochin, Cananor, and Ormuz, deposing unfaithful or rebellious governors, putting the administration in order, and replacing bad officials with good ones. Had Vasco da Gama lived in this age and in America, he would have been called a model "civil-service reformer."

It is probable, that, for a man of his age, his labors were excessive. Before he had been in India three months, he was attacked by illness, which at first, however, did not seem serious. He felt severe pains in the neck; and boils broke out upon him, and tormented him so that he was unable to turn his head on one side or the other. These attacks made him irritable. The grave cares of his office, which always filled his thoughts, only increased his pains. He was at Cochin, a town on the Indian coast south of Calicut, when this illness overtook him. Finding that it grew more serious, he caused himself to be conveyed from the fort to the house of a Portuguese gentleman near by. He still attempted to exercise his authority as viceroy; but, feeling that his end might be near, he sent for various officers, and gave them orders what to do if he should die. He made the treasurer and secretary sign a promise to do all that he commanded until his successor should arrive, and had his instructions to them carefully written out in full.

Having thus disposed of his worldly affairs, Don Vasco da Gama turned his thoughts to higher and more solemn things, and prepared himself for death, which was now fast approaching. He made his will, confessed, and partook of the holy sacrament. In his will he enjoined upon his sons Estevan and Paulo to return to Portugal, and carry with them his goods and his servants, paying those who wished to remain in India what was due to them; to give his clothes and household furniture to the churches and the hospital; and to see to it that his remains should be conveyed to and entombed in his native land.

Gradually, day by day, the old hero failed; until,

at three o'clock in the morning, on Christmas Eve, 1524, he quietly passed away.

The news of his death filled the Portuguese in India with grief. The churches were crowded with those who repaired to them to pray for the rest of his soul. His body, clad in silk attire, and wrapped in the mantle of the Order of Christ, lay in state in the hall of the fortress. On his head was the round cap that he had been wont to wear on state occasions, while by his side were laid his sword and belt. From the fortress the remains were carried to the Monastery of St. Antony, and deposited in the large chapel. A square grating surrounded the tomb, which was lined with fringed black velvet. The next day a mass for the repose of the illustrious dead was said, attended by Don Vasco's two sons as chief mourners, and by all the high officers and captains who were at Cochin. Some years after, his body was taken from its resting-place in Cochin, and carried back to Portugal in the admiral's flagship, and interred amid great splendor at Vidigueyra, the town from which he derived his title; and there he lies to this day. Don Vasco's sons fulfilled their father's commands in every respect. When they returned home with the sad news, all Portugal mourned so great and irreparable a loss.

Thus died this celebrated hero, captain, governor, and patriot, after a life full of adventure, and crowned with all the fame and honors that the most ambitious could crave. Vasco da Gama had faults: his temper was quick and hot, his manner and action often arbitrary, his severity sometimes cruel. On the other hand, he was bold, persevering, patient of fatigue, disdainful of danger and of obstacles, prompt in executing justice, religious, devoted to his king and country, and full of the most untiring energy. Such a memory the Portuguese may well be proud to cherish, and preserve to the homage of future generations.